The Scattered Autumn Leaves

A Memoir

A desperate flight during the last months of World War II

By Aurelia Gincauskas

Copyright © 2017 Aurelia Gincauskas

All rights reserved under International and Pan-American conventions.

No part of this book may be used or reproduced without written permission from the author, except in the case of quotations from reviews.

First Edition

July 2016

ISBN-13: 978-1545304532

ISBN-10: 154530453

Book & Cover Design: Robison Design

Printed in the USA

Dedication

To my dear mother Michalina whose strength and resilience I admire.

In memory of Bronius, my father and

Stasys, my uncle.

Contents

	About The Author	i
	Prologue	iii
I	Sensation of Doom	1
II	Parent's Farm	9
III	Time Of Reflection	17
IV	Walk Through the Woods	23
V	Decision Made	29
VI	Flight	35
VII	The German-Russian Front	43
VIII	The Barn In Prussia	49
IX	Flight to the Nemunas River	55
X	The Nemunas River	63
XI	Tilsit	71
XII	Kaliningrad	77
XIII	Vienna	83

XIV	Stockerau	93
XV	Lovely Room	101
XVI	A New Friend	105
XVII	The Bully	109
XVIII	Caught	115
XIX	A Train Full of Soldiers	123
XX	Ghostly Terrain	129
XXI	Kempten	133
XXII	Life In The D.P. Camp	143
XXIII	The Last Train	155
	Historical Points of Interest	163
	Epilogue	167
	Author's Personal Story	171
	Acknowledgements	175

About The Author

I am a child of Lithuanian immigrant parents who fled their country to escape the invading Red Army. My mother was into her first month of pregnancy when their flight began on October 6, 1944. They faced horrific moments and witnessed many human tragedies while dodging bombardments during their flight. Nine months later, two days after the war ended, I was born in a Southern German town called Kempten 60 miles southwest of Munich. The first words my mother asked the nurse after my birth is "Is my baby normal?"

And so I began my first four years of life in a world that was torn and ripped apart by War. I have been having certain memories or images from those years in Germany throughout my life and recently they have been surfacing more frequently. Images of playing with little girls in the ruins of a disheveled landscape. Images of a very old smiling, gentle lady with white hair sitting in the center of an empty dark room with outstretched arms towards me while I am holding my mother's hand; Images of me sitting on a bench in a cemetery watching my mother place a small bunch of daisies next to a tiny rectangular stone; Images of looking up toward a open gnarling mouth of a large iron lion.

Since these memories of my very early youth keep surfacing, I feel a need to reflect on a life I lived. And so, I begin to explore the beginning from where I had emerged before I write my story in the future.

Prologue

This is a story about three young people Michalina, her husband Bronius, and his brother Stasys who were caught in the middle of two large armies, the retreating German army and the advancing Red army. Memory of the cruel Russian occupation in the early part of the war in 1940-41 was still fresh in their minds. They could either stay with the danger of being and be killed or deported to Siberia. Fearing for their lives they decided to flee their homeland of Lithuania

There is a nation by the Baltic Sea whose existence was acknowledged in written documents 1009 AD. As a warrior state the small nation conquered neighboring lands and became the Grand Duchy of Lithuania in 13th century. In the next couple centuries Lithuania expanded to extend from the Baltic Sea to the Black Sea. It was the last areas in

Europe to adopt Christianity (early 14th century) and became the largest state in Europe in the 15th century. Lithuania united with Poland in the 16th century and ruled as Lithuanian-Poland Commonwealth for the next two hundred years. Lithuania-Poland disappeared as a nation when Czarist Russian rule took it over in the late 18th century.

After World War I Lithuania, which then became just a small "thumb print" on the map by the Baltic Sea, finally acquired their independence as a democratic state on February 16th, 1918 for the next 22 years. In the early years of World War II the country was forcefully occupied by Russia after an infamous pact, the Molotov-Ribbentrop Pact, the Russians made with the Nazi government. From 1940-1941 the Russian regime ruled Lithuania with a cruel vengeance deporting 60,000 citizens to Siberia where many died because of the hardships of life in the harsh terrain. Many of the deported citizens were from the intelligentsia class, landowners, and priests. When Nazi Germany attacked the Russians, they became the occupiers from 1941-1945.

In the early autumn of 1944, The Russian army advanced toward the Baltic countries as the weary German Army retreated. The memory of the cruel Russian occupation in 1940-1941 panicked everyone as the Russian army advanced toward the cities. Many citizens fled.

Detail Of The Flight In Lithuania

Starting in Telsiai they took the train to Kretinga, Silute, Tilsit to Kaliningrad.

Flight Across Europe

Starting in Kaliningrad they took the train to Vienna.
Four months later they took the train to Kempten where they lived in the Displaced Persons Camps for four years.
They then took the train to Bremen where they boarded the Sea Marlin, a U.S. Navy ship.

Chapter I

§

Sensation Of Doom

September 5th, 1945 a beautiful autumn day embraced a small city by a lake. The sun shone brilliantly, lighting up the colorful foliage of oranges, yellows and reds. Spider webs entwined between the branches of many sidewalk shrubs captured the sun's rays giving an illusion of millions of sparkling diamonds entrapped in the silvery fragile threads. Such was the day that Michalina took a walk. And yet on such a magnificent day doom etched peoples' faces as they rushed to their destinations oblivious to the surrounding beauty of their city, Telsiai. Muffled explosions boomed in the distance announcing the invading army's approach. Sounds of war were very frightening.

Twenty-four year old Michalina a slim lovely woman with hazel eyes and soft long brown hair clutched her sweater close to her throat as the cool autumn breeze brushed against her face. The heavy feeling in her chest increased as she sensed people rushing by with their heads bent down and eyebrows furrowed in horror. The Russian front approached. Their small country capital, Vilnius, was captured on July 23, 1944 and the provisional capital Kaunas was taken on August 1st. Now the Russian army was sixty miles away. Suddenly, Michalina had an urge to rush home. What will happen to her war torn county? What will happen to her life? She married a handsome son of a landowner, and lived comfortably in a three room apartment brick duplex two blocks from the city's railroad station. Her husband Bronius has been the head stationmaster for two years.

As Michalina approached home her neighbor Mr. Barkus smiled and waved and she acknowledged him with a nod. She sadly gazed at the lush green yard where her grey cow, Melene lazily grazed. Her father-in-law gave her the cow as a wedding gift, and this was a luxury since fresh milk was difficult to obtain. Michalina absently glanced at her vegetable garden. The row of tomato plants appeared tired with withering leaves and a few ripe fruits ready to be plucked. She picked up a small spade and approached the potato plant. As the spade stabbed the soft earth revealing a few potato roots ready to be harvested, Michalina realized that her effort was useless since they will not need this now. Nevertheless, she placed the potatoes in a basket and brought them into the kitchen. She was deep in thought when she became startled by a figure sitting in the room past the kitchen.

"Stasys, you startled me! What are you doing home so early?" she inquired.

Stasys was her brother-in-law who lived with them. Housing was very difficult to obtain and expensive. Michalina did not mind since he was quiet and helpful around the house. He also worked in a food warehouse that allowed him to bring home precious meats and sausages, rare in a war torn country. Since there was only one bedroom in the household, Stasys slept on the couch in the sitting room.

"We were told to leave early because of the bombing, and besides, I was looking forward to relax before Bronius came home," he said smiling sheepishly.

"I am anxious about these bombings," Michalina helplessly explained, "They are coming closer and closer. There is a feeling of apprehension in this entire city. Most of the inhabitants have fled the country this past month. And here we sit." she completed her sentence with a sigh.

"We will wait and discuss that with Bronius" Stasys responded.

He always relied on his older brother for advice even though he disliked Bronius' habit of continuously giving orders to him. Stasys was a tall and handsome fellow with dark hair, high cheekbones, and a sheepish smile. He was not aggressive like his brother. He enjoyed drinking with his friends and playing basketball. Stasys was the son his father loved the best.

Suddenly the door opened with a jolt. Stasys and Michalina jumped.

"I am hungry! What are we eating tonight?" Bronius impatiently asked.

Michalina looked at her husband annoyingly. He always wanted things done immediately.

"How could you think of food at a time like this. The Russians are sixty miles away from our city," she angrily retorted.

"You need your energy for running," Bronius teased. "Besides, I heard the news from the station that the Germans were pushing the Russians back," he reassured us. "I suggest that we stay with my parents for two weeks since I have some time off," he continued.

His boss was a mild mannered German who did like Bronius and usually granted any of his requests.

"Are you sure this is wise?" she questioned.

She wanted to believe him since he sounded so

convincing, standing there in the doorway wearing a handsome khaki long coat and slacks over which he wore his long black shining boots, and a captain's hat tilted to one side. That is how he looked when she first met him in the cafeteria at the railroad station.

There was talk among the women that a handsome bachelor is the new head stationmaster. While working at the cafeteria as a waitress she noticed him in the food line and her first impressions were not good. He was dashing and good looking, but he was boastful, loud, conceited, and noticed that he had a roving eye for any lady that passed him. In a half a year, alas, she succumbed to his congenial side and married him. They were married in a civil ceremony at a courthouse not far from the small chapel by the lake. Michalina's parents and siblings could not make the long difficult journey. Bronius introduced his future bride to his parents a few weeks before they were married. He asked his father to buy the two gold wedding bands. His father abruptly refused. However, two weeks after the wedding his father organized a wedding party with pastries and meats difficult to get during the war. It was a wonderful surprise for Michalina and she felt welcomed into the family.

"Yes, I think we should go and decide with our parents what we should do," answered Bronius firmly. So that ended their discussion.

Michalina's Choral Group, 1938

Michalina Seated first row, left with her choral group in her village of Pavandene, Lithuania. Her older sister, Sofija stands on the far left. Elze the younger sister sits in the second row, third from left

Bronius' Graduation Class 1938 Having Fun
Bronius stands in upper row, right side with Handkerchief on his head

Chapter II

§

Parents' Farm

Hello kids! Welcome, welcome! bellowed Michalina's father-in-law with arms outstretched toward the three weary travelers who walked fifteen miles to reach their ancestral farm.

Michalina waved happily at the fatherly figure whose bulky body appeared massive in the doorway. Legs wide apart and hands on his waist, he appeared genuinely happy to see them. His smile showed off gleaming teeth framed by a massive graying curly beard and moustache. Michalina was glad to see him. Even though he was extremely stingy with his money, he was always willing to help anyone with a dilemma. His eighty-acre apple and cherry orchard farm was beautifully arranged and the house he built was large and comfortable. In the past he maintained eight exquisite horses, which were confiscated by the German army. Under the Nazi occupation for past two years, farmers were forced to provide certain quota of produce for them. Severe consequences occurred if the quotas were short. Rumor was that the poor farmers were hanged when quotas were not met.

"Come in, Come in." he said as he embraced Michalina and scrutinized her face as he led her to the parlor.

His brow wrinkled as he saw her frail nervous appearance. Bronius and Stasys kicked of their boots and sat down with a sigh. At this moment Michalina's mother-in-law walked in briskly carrying a basket of eggs, which she had collected from their chickens. Elated in seeing her two sons, she dashed to embrace them in tears. The brothers eagerly returned her embraces. She was a quiet and kind woman with dark circles around her eyes and her grey hair was severely stretched back into a bun. There was a glimmer of an impression that she was once a beautiful woman.

"We want to stay a while and to discuss the

threatened arrival of the Russians." Bronius interrupted his weeping mother.

"Well son," said Michalina's father-in-law, as he sat heavily on the dining room chair and crossing his hands in front, "I feel the Germans are being pushed back. I know this because many partisans are organizing to fight against the approaching Russian army. I feel that the end is truly here."

He finished the last sentence in a slow harsh whisper as he gazed teary eyed into the distance. He sustained his gaze for a minute as if he was reviewing his entire past struggling life. As a young man he came to America and became a police officer in Boston. Being homesick after ten years he returned to his homeland of Lithuania. He married a wealthy landowner's daughter, acquired land and started establish his orchards.

Then World War I started. Times were hard and dangerous and continued to be unstable even after the Lithuanian Declaration of Independence on February 16th, 1918. The Czarist government had fallen and the Bolsheviks occupied his city Siauliai forcefully in the winter of 1919. Fortunately, the Lithuanian resistance forces successfully defended their country and the Lithuanian-Russian negotiations ended favorably. The Baltic coastline was free from the Bolsheviks. Then in the summer of 1919 the Germans began evacuating Lithuania. Bronius, his first was born then. He smiled, thinking about his difficult mischievous son. Then came the great years of independence.

"These were great happy years that we had," he whispered softly under his breath.

"Father, are you alright?" Stasys asked as he embraced his father's shoulders.

This interrupted his thoughts immediately jolted him back to the present as his teary eyes focused on his concerned family members eying him intently. He smiled sadly while patting his younger son's hand.

"We face hard times in this country and there will be no guarantee that we shall be free after this hellish war," he said with a firm strong voice and continued. "In the past four years we have been occupied first by the Russian terror with deportations of our people," saying this he banged his fist on the table, "and now the German terror," again banging his fist on the table. He scanned his audience slowly and deliberately. "The Russian army is marching here again and they will show no mercy. My advice to you, my dear children, is to…" he paused before completing his sentence. "My advice is to run."

"Noooo, no!" cried his wife grabbing Stasys close to her bosom.

"Run, my children, before the Russian front engulfs you!" he continued overriding his wife's agonized weeping.

Michalina glanced over to the stunned faces of her husband and brother-in-law. Obviously, this was not the advice they expected to hear.

"Mother will prepare us a fine dinner," he said breaking the silence.

Approaching his crying wife, with a smile he gently coaxed her. She wiped her eyes with a linen handkerchief, blew her nose and started toward the kitchen.

"We would like to stay here for a few days so we could absorb your point of view father." Bronius said as he paced back and forth with his head down and hands clasped in front.

His father's advice agitated him. Michalina recalled that he was not concerned about the war and felt that Lithuania would return to its pre-war independent state.

"Well!" boomed the father half jovially slapping both hands on the table trying to jolt his sons from their shock. "I'm happy that you are here, so at least let us share these precious moments to enjoy each others company for the next few days. Mother will take care of us very well." he winked at his stunned sons.

Gincauskas Family Farm Near Telsiai, Lithuania, 1934
Mounted on horses: Bronius, left and Stasys, right.
Their sister Brone gives flowers to Bronius. Parents stand in the center.

Bronius Graduation Class, 1938
Bronius is seated in the first row, third from left.

Chapter III

§

Time Of Reflection

The two weeks in September at Michalina's father-in-law's farm were very happy. Michalina spent many hours with him talking about his sons, his experiences in America, and his ambitions of being a large orchard farmer and horse rancher. He nurtured eight beautiful horses before the Nazis confiscated them. Now only one remained for transportation. In the past year, he frequently visited us in Telsiai. Bells on his magnificent horses hitched to the sleigh announced his arrival. They were heard for miles around. Michalina remembered the thrill and excitement when he lent his horses and sleigh for their enjoyment. She and Bronius would anxiously climb in, drape the warm woolen blankets over their knees and gallop with the sounds of jingles filling the air as her father-in-law watched proudly with his hands on his waist, legs parted, wearing a long furry coat, which made his massive body even more bulky. Coming from a very poor family, these moments made Michalina feel like a grand lady.

"How is Bronius treating you?" he asked Michalina one day.

His sons just left to complete various farm chores. As usual Bronius always moaned and grumbled when he had to do manual labor. Michalina paused before answering because he was indeed a difficult man to live with. But she still loved him.

"You don't have to answer the question," her father-in-law said quickly, noticing her pause. Michalina opened her mouth to say that she was fine, but he interrupted her by raising his hand to signal that he wishes to complete his thoughts. "I love both of my sons dearly, but Bronius is the most difficult son to deal with. He is lazy and always tries to get out of any work. He always made his younger brother do his work."

Michalina chuckled under her breath because she saw this in her household while Stasys was living with them. Bronius did like one thing, Michalina thought. He loved to flirt with women. She recalled the visit with her family in their town, Pavandene after their marriage. The little village where Michalina was born was thirty miles south from Telsiai. Since the roads were very bad and rarely used, the journey lasted all night with their borrowed horse and buggy. Michalina anticipated introducing her husband to her mother, however, to her irritation, Bronius spent all day flirting with her three giggling sisters. He was not paying any attention to my prim and proper mother who, Michalina noticed, was getting more agitated by her fast talking husband.

"I feel that your marriage will not last long." She told Michalina as they hugged before their long journey back to Telsiai. Her quiet diplomatic father kissed her.

"You will be fine," he said patting her hand gently.

As the carriage jerked forward and increased the momentum, she turned to throw kisses at the diminishing figures of her family standing by the little one room house, where Michalina was born, waving their good-byes. At that point a strange feeling gripped her heart. Will this be the last image of her family?

"And do you know what your son-of-a-bitch husband did with my money," boomed Michalina's father-in-law, jerking her back to the present with a jump.

"What did he do," she asked meekly, not being certain if she wanted to hear any more.

"I gave Stasys and Bronius each one thousand litas to pay for their education in Siauliai. This would have provided books and six months of room and board. My good son Stasys deposited all his money in the bank and he was very thrifty." After an angry pause, remembering that event, he continued, "But Bronius spend all his money in two weeks to stay in luxurious hotels and go to fancy nightclubs!"

Her father-in-law paused again as he wiped his lips with his handkerchief. Clearly he was very irritated at the memory. Michalina recalled her husband boasting about his escapades. With the money Bronius received from his father for his education, he instead bought an expensive suit, wide brim fashionable hat, and leather gloves. He and a friend, who he claimed was more handsome than himself, visited all the expensive and fashionable restaurants and nightclubs at a resort city. This was a beautiful seaside Baltic vacation site where all the wealthy people and politicians spent their summer holidays. The intent of these two dashing men was to impress beautiful women. Two weeks of good times passed and so did all his money, while Stasys'- money remained safely in the bank. However, an irony had occurred. Stasys' money was also liquidated. Early in the war the Russians forcefully took over Lithuania after the pact with Germany on March 25th 1940, the currency litas of independent Lithuania was no longer legal and was replaced by the ruble. Bronius tantalized his younger brother about this.

"You see, my dear brother, we both lost our money. At least I have a new wardrobe and a memory of a rich time on the Baltic seaside," he annoyingly teased him. "Grab the moment now," he used to advise his brother. "For the future might not promise you anything."

Two weeks passed pleasantly at the farm. The time to depart cruelly arrived. Michalina's weeping mother-in-law was busily packing the baskets with eggs, meats, and breads for the journey. Silently they packed their meager belongings. The painful hour arrived as all sadly hugged and kissed.

"Notify us when you will be fleeing" urged Bronius' father. "Be cautious and don't trust anyone," he advised somberly. The father watched sadly with his weeping wife at his side, as the figures of his sons and daughter-in-law disappeared into the forest. "Goodbye, my sons, goodbye," his trembling lips whispered.

•

Chapter IV

§

Walk Through The Woods

The three figures were walking through quiet birch forest and the silence was only interrupted by their footsteps rustling the leaves and cracking the twigs on the soft forest ground. Their thoughts were occupied by the father's opinion urging them to flee. Bronius mumbled under his breath as he quickened his pace. Deep in thought he paid no attention to his wife and brother who were trying to keep up with him.

"Hold on Bronius," Stasys urged him breathing heavily. "Can't talk with you while your running. What did you think of father's advice?" He anxiously asked.

"What do you think," Bronius snapped back. "We will have to leave quickly." Bronius continued his fast pace leaving his astonished brother behind. Michalina quickly ran to him and grabbed for his hand and squeezed it.

"Are you alright?" she asked concerned with his worried expression, since she rarely saw him genuinely concerned.

"I was just thinking about father." he slowly responded. "I'll really miss him," he said softly squeezing his wife's hand gently. "I know that he was always disappointed with me," he continued. "He always shouted at me for doing this or not doing that. I was thinking about the time when I was eight years old. I was instructed to take the cows to pasture for the day. I borrowed my father's expensive knife before leading the cattle to the grazing field. He did warn me not to loose it. I fell asleep on the grass and when I awoke it was time to bring the cows back to the stable. But to my dismay, I noticed that the knife was missing." Bronius paused as if he felt that moment of fear again. "I searched frantically for my father's knife without success. I fell to my knees and prayed intensely to the Blessed Virgin Mary to help me find the knife." Bronius paused for a longer time reliving that moment again. Impatiently Michalina urged him to go on.

"What happened, Bronius? Did you find the knife?" Jerked back to the present Bronius sighed.

"I did not find it and resigned to come home empty handed and face the consequences from my father. As I led the cows to the stable I noticed something gleaming in the muddy path by the gate. I bent down to see better and lo and behold, it was the knife! I was so overjoyed that I dropped on my knees on the mud to thank the Virgin Mary for saving me from my father's scolding. In the eyes of a young boy I truly believed this was a miracle!" Bronius looked at Michalina and smiled. "What happened most likely is that the knife was caught in one of the hooves of the cow and was dislodged by the gate. But I never forgot that time. Father was such a disciplinarian and when he approached me when I misbehaved he looked threatening as if he would strike at me. You know, I used show fear and hold my head and cry, but I knew that there was no threat. I knew that he loved my brother and me very much." Bronius paused again and Michalina waited patiently for him to reflect about the memory of his father. "I resolved to be a priest for many years because of this miracle," he chuckled.

"You a priest!" laughed Michalina visualizing him chasing all the cute women in his parish.

"As a teenager I thought that it would be a great profession. A priest lives in a manor and always has an adoring crowd."

"Yah, but you cannot be married or be with women," Michalina joked.

"Who said that? No one has to know what a priest does in private," Bronius replied with a quick wink. They all continued to walk in silence towards Telsiai not knowing what lay ahead of them.

Juozas Gincauskas, 1947

Bronius' and Stasys' father

Chapter V

§

Decision Made

The two weeks that had passed in Telsiai were very hectic. Bronius worked double shifts since extra trains brought German soldiers and military equipment into the city. There were rumors that the Russians broke the German line about sixty miles southeast of Telsiai and were marching northward. This was certainly a very uncomfortable feeling since there was so little time to organize for a quick flight from the city. Michalina and the two men constantly discussed the question of preparing for their flight westward toward the Baltic coast forty miles away and then southward ten miles to the port of Klaipeda and another thirty miles to Silute near the Nemunas River.

Bronius hastily returned from work to inform Michalina that the Russians were nearing the railroad station.

"Stay here," he demanded. "I'm required to complete my work at the station due to the added railroad responsibilities. This way I will be able to get seats on the last train tomorrow."

"Tomorrow," gasped Michalina, interrupting Bronius' pacing. "What about my parents?" She passionately recalled her last image of them standing by her birthplace.

"They live to far Michalina," he said softly. "We do not have the time. Our life depends on how soon we can get the hell out of here. Those are the facts that we must accept." Bronius paused and again observed Michalina's acceptance of the desperate situation.

"Stasys knows what to do. As soon as he arrives you both run quickly to the farm and hug my parents for me." He kissed her and ran out the door.

Within two hours Michalina and Stasys reached her father-in-law's farm. Michalina saw the farmhouse standing serenely in the distance framed in back with beautiful rows of orchards. A field of tall grass surrounded the house as a gentle warm autumn breeze swayed the blades in rhythmic waves and the bright yellow autumn birch leaves were waiting for the wind to nudge them for a descent. A tiny figure hunched down in the garden adjacent to the house. Her father-in-law slowly lifted his head seeing the two approaching figures. Slowly he straightened his body and waited. Michalina quickened her pace, then stopped abruptly in front of him. His face was drawn accentuating his deep grooves and his eyes reflected agony. He knew why they arrived. After the brief moment of the silent realization, they dashed into each other's arms and sobbed.

Stasys approached his father's side consoling him. His father turned to his younger son and cuffed Stasys' face with his large rough hands and kissed his cheeks repeatedly as if this was their last meeting. They all slowly approached the doorway where the distraught mother was waiting as she clutched her linen apron.

They spent two hours sadly discussing the flight, while Michalina's mother-in-law slowly packed their basket with fresh eggs and meats all the while weeping softly as she wiped her eyes intermittently with her beige linen apron.

"We will return soon after the war," promised Michalina. "This tyrannical disruption of our life will not last forever." Michalina's father-in-law patted her on the hand and smiled. His sad eyes and furrowed brow told a different future.

"It's getting late and you had better be on your way back," he said with an urgent sigh as he stood up from the table. "I'll go and hitch the horse to the buggy and take you home so you can get there sooner."

Michalina leaned against the doorway while watching her beloved in-law preparing the horse for their journey. Stasys remained in the house consoling his crying mother. Michalina's thoughts resided now with her parents. She was greatly saddened because she was unable to say good-bye to them. When the buggy was ready, her mother-in-law placed the egg laden basket in the back of the buggy, kissed us again before we mounted, and said as she wiped off the tears from her cheeks.

"Perhaps I shall never see you again."

Before Stasys and Michalina could say anything, the buggy jerked forward and picked up speed. They could only wave at the lonely diminishing figures in the field of undulating long grass.

As soon as they entered the birch forest with its colorful yellow foliage, three planes dropped low and suddenly started to shoot. Terrified, they all jumped out of the buggy and ran to the nearest cluster of trees for shelter.

"These are Russian planes," said Stasys, shutting his eyes tight when again the swooping planes fired continuous shots. "The German army is probably not far from here," he continued when the shooting subsided.

After ten minutes of shooting complete silence engulfed the forest once more. Michalina's father-in-law's expression was distorted with widened eyes and open mouth while his hands cupped his face as they rushed toward the frightened horse. Michalina's knees were extremely so weak she leaned against the wagon to stay standing. Her eyes focused on the broken eggs that spilled on the buggy's floor, displaying the gelatinous albumin and golden yolks. The scene mesmerized her for a moment as if she was in a gallery observing a still life painting. A harsh distant voice slowly broke her trance.

"The eggs are cracked!" Michalina quickly recovered and again heard her father-in-law's nervous comment. "It's a shame that mother gave these eggs and now they are all broken. Now my horse is in danger of being shot," he lamented stroking his agitated animal's nose. "I cannot allow this." He continued while mounting his wagon. He paused and stepped down again and hugged Stasys. "You had better walk quickly through the forest without my guidance."

He embarked clumsily on the wagon and drove away with the broken eggs, as Michalina and Stasys blankly starred. Michalina's lips twisted into a sarcastic smile watching her father-in-law driving away.

"He is more concerned about his horse being shot than us," she said bitterly.

Stasys shuffled uncomfortably and slowly responded, "Michalina, we are under a lot of stress. Father's actions are justified. The horse is his only means of transportation."

As they continued their journey through the forest, Michalina meditated deeply. Her thoughts were on war. The gathering of stormy clouds of war produced such sad and incongruous situations in human emotion. Life must go on she thought, while the war is passing through. Avoid its path, dodge it, and hide from it the best way possible, or else, you will be left behind under its grip.

Chapter VI

§

Flight

Michalina and Stasys were terrified of whom they may encounter as they dashed through the forest. Dusk had arrived when they entered their room, and found Bronius anxiously awaiting them.

"What happened?" he asked noticing their disheveled appearance. "Did you encounter any trouble?"

Stasys answered sitting down wearily on the chair, "It appeared that we were near a German patrol since the Russian planes were shooting in our vicinity. We were in the wagon with father…"

"With father? Was he injured?" interrupted Bronius anxiously.

"We all survived other than our fragile nerves," Stasys said.

"Bronius, when are we leaving?" Michalina pleaded approaching him face to face.

"Tomorrow I'll know better," he said as he kissed his trembling wife on the forehead.

That night, they tried to sleep but sleep was constantly interrupted by distant tanks bellowing fiery shots. Since their nerves were on edge, Bronius dressed up early, and prepared to leave.

"I'm going to the station to inquire about the approaching front," he said to Michalina who sat at the edge of the bed bracing herself against the bedpost.

"I will be back soon," he said disappearing through the doorway.

Michalina's aching body slowly raised and she proceeded towards the sitting room. Stasys blankly stared through the window. The sun was just peaking over the horizon. Distracted, Stasys then turned his head, to watch Michalina prepare breakfast. She appeared taunt from a restless evening. His preoccupation was centered on what uncomfortable news his brother might bring. Bronius returned shortly appearing rushed and agitated.

"The Russian front is about fifteen miles from here," he said breathlessly. "All the German workers are leaving on the last train in five hours."

"What about us?" Stasys nervously interrupted.

"The station master provided us with three seats. We have five hours to prepare for our departure." Bronius hesitated and added, "We must travel light with only one suitcase. I have to return to the station and finish my work." Bronius departed quickly. Stasys picked up his jacket and turned around at the doorway to look at Michalina who stood immobilized in the center of the room.

"I'm going to say goodbye to my friends," Stasys said as he closed the door behind him.

Michalina sighed and proceeded to search for appropriate clothing for their flight, still in shock with the facts Bronius presented to her. She started slowly and carefully to collect her articles until distant shots of war interrupted her intensity. She increased her pace by just scooping all the clothing from the drawer. As she did this, she brushed against her picture album, which was hidden beneath her underwear. She slowly picked up the shabby grey album with frayed edges, sat down on the couch, and gently and thoughtfully turned the pages.

Before her eyes flashed her childhood years. There were photos of her classmates posing for a school portrait with sheepish grins, photos of her sisters laughing while there arms are clasped at the elbow and pictures of her parents always posing formally. Michalina smiled sadly at picture of her mother sitting rigidly straight, her hair drawn severely back, and the long black dress carefully hiding her ankles, as her father stood tall next to her. Michalina gently touched the picture as tears swelled in her eyes. The last page contained a few pictures of her and Bronius standing by the chapel after their wedding. Then the handsome portrait of Bronius wearing his fashionable wide brim hat and expensive suit was pasted on the last grey page of the album. Michalina laugh softly as she realized the Baltic seaside resort took this portrait during his infamous time. Bronius wanted to remember the moment.

Shutting the album she placed it in the bottom of the suitcase. All the odds and ends of essentials packed, Michalina dressed in a grey traveling suit and sturdy brown leather boots. She gathered the remaining few morsels of the sausages and bread, wrapped them in newspaper, and placed that in the suitcase too. As Michalina was fastening the lid, Stasys walked in.

"I gave our cow to the next door neighbor, and told them that we are leaving today. They were extremely grateful," Stasys said.

"Oh, Melene, I completely forgot about her!" Michalina exclaimed remembering that gentle beast that provided them with plentiful milk.

"It's almost three o'clock Michalina, Bronius is waiting for us at the station," Stasys said as he picked up the suitcase. They both walked out without looking back.

The railroad station buzzed with chaos. Confused people scurried to find seats on trains. Shouts of German orders and direction boomed through loudspeakers. Michalina spotted her husband standing by one of the railcars waving frantically to catch their attention. He wore his khaki uniform and boots that were still surprisingly polished and shiny.

"There are three seats in this car second row from the right. Be seated now before we lose them in this confusion," he implored.

Michalina and Stasys strained their necks to find and empty seat in the crowded car. An elderly man who appeared befuddled was heading for an empty seat. Michalina rushed by him and seated herself by the window placing her gloves on the two remaining seats. The elderly gentleman paused and focusing intently on her gloves then headed onward. Stasys followed him and sat next to Michalina grinning accusingly at her.

"I know that was rude," she said without any feeling of guilt. "We have to be aggressive in times like these." She noted Stasys' upward rolling eyes. "Well, did you want us to loose our seats?" Michalina snapped at him turning her head away from him. "Well, Michalina, you're beginning to act like Bronius." she muttered to herself.

Gazing through the window she watched German soldiers cram into the other cars. Civilians kissed friends and tearful relatives. Others, carrying their crying children tried to enter other coaches. Michalina glanced at the railroad clock over the entrance of the station and, too her surprise, an hour and forty-five minutes had passed. She became slightly agitated and wondered where her husband was and why the train wasn't moving by now. Sounds of bombing and shooting definitely approached their city. When she saw Bronius struggle through the aisle to reach them Michalina felt relief and her body slightly relaxed.

"Push the window down, Michalina," Bronius said.

Michalina wrinkled her nose in a puzzled expression and jerked the window down. Beneath the window, they were greeted by their smiling neighbor, Mrs. Barkus, who handed her a large bowl of steaming cabbage soup with sausage.

"In gratitude for such a precious gift, your cow, I'm bringing you something to eat. You must surely be hungry by now," she said with exuberance.

They all thanked her profusely as Michalina reached down to receive her soup and in minutes all three of them noisily devoured the liquid. The train finally jerked westward at five o'clock, on October 9th, 1944. The train's whistling and rhythmic chugging competed with the sounds of the approaching artillery. Michalina closed her eyes. Their flight had begun.

Chapter VII

§

The German-Russian Front

The train screeched to a stop sixty miles later at Kretinga, a few miles away from the Baltic resort city of Palanga. Distant air raids wailed followed by bursts of explosions and shots. An hour later, the train had not budged. Michalina was too tired to be afraid. She sensed the restlessness of people in the car as Bronius and Stasys whispered. Her feet ached in her boots. She struggled to remove them as her eyelids were closing. She yearned to sleep and nothing was going to stop her. Michalina slid to the floor, placed her head on her suitcase and disappeared into a deep dream.

Unaware of where her legs were taking her Michalina found herself running in a dark wet forest and hearing only her heavy labored breathing. Bony branches of sinister trees seemed to reach for her as she frantically brushed them away dodging their reach. The rain became heavier slashing against her face as she ran deeper into the forest. Michalina gasped as she turned around feeling pursued. She tried harder to run faster but her body did not respond to her desperate need. Suddenly, her foot caught a root of a tree causing her to tumble and role off the edge of a deep gully. Her body rolled down over the soggy ground as the smell of wet dry leaves, bark, and soil penetrated her nostrils. Her wilted body jerked to a stop. Her eyes widened, focusing on a tipped basket of broken eggs, with their golden yolks coalescing on the wet soil in front of her. She gasped as flashes of lightening and thunder exploded in the atmosphere.

A deafening explosion jolted her awake. Panic gripped the cabin as shouting and crying people scurried out. Michalina groped for her boots with trembling hands as she heard Bronius' urging voice.

"Michalina, get up quickly. We got to get out of here. We've been hit!"

Michalina was stunned and could not move until she put on her boots. Two more explosions boomed in succession vigorously shaking the car. Michalina let out a scream and ran out compressing her ears tightly with her hands. She jumped out into the hazy darkness with the pungent smoke burning her nostrils. Jumping into a ditch to escape the flying shrapnel Michalina saw Bronius and Stasys on their stomachs with their arms covering their heads. In the darkness terrifying explosions and machine gun fire spewed over their heads as they ducked for safety in the ditch. All Michalina could do was pray for their survival. An hour passed but it seemed like an eternity. Then the shooting ceased, uncovering human sounds of agony. Moans, weeping, and weak voices pleading for help echoed in the night. Michalina cautiously stood up with everyone in the ditch as Bronius squeezed her hand in tribute to their miraculous survival. A horrible scene of many twisted immobile bodies lay ahead of them. A completely charred young German soldier was being consoled in the arms of another soldier. As Michalina passed the dying soldier, she saw the lips of his charred face move.

"Please, tell my mother that I love her," the soldier whispered with his last breath as he faded away and became still with his head resting against his crying comrade's arms.

Michalina walked past the corpses in a trance and followed Bronius and Stasys through the disoriented crowds who were immobilized by this attack. Bronius abruptly stopped her.

"Look, our cabin is totally destroyed!" Bronius exclaimed and turned to them as if he discovered a fact. "We would have certainly been killed."

Michalina shuddered as every muscle in her bodied tightened and prepared to sprint at any other oncoming danger. She was in on a survival mode.

At ten o'clock the chilly night breeze pierced Michalina's body as they huddled together on the ground amid death and destruction. As the last flickering flame of a bombed railcar was extinguished and the bodies buried, people gathered in groups to discuss their next move. Bronius circulated among the crowds of civilians and soldiers to get more information and found out that another train would arrive soon. Michalina realized that they were stranded at the German-Russian front with no food, shelter, nor clothing. Rumor spread like wildfire. One said they were totally surrounded by the Russian Army. Also the German soldiers were unsuccessful in stopping the aggressive advance of the Russian military. The desperate crowd sighed of temporary relief and cheered as an approaching train whistle screamed in the distance. When the train arrived, crowds of people frantically rushed toward the coaches pushing and shoving to get in. Fortunately, Bronius pushed his way the hardest and managed to pull Michalina up with him into the coach. After they were seated comfortably, Michalina looked around to find Stasys and spotted him safely standing at the end of the aisle. She was so relieved to see that he managed to get into the train car through the desperate crowd of passengers. He always disliked shoving and pushing.

Slowly the train started to move. An eerie silence enveloped the coach. People appeared as apparitions blankly looking at the passing landscape, all yearning for a safe haven for their families. Hope soon shattered when the train suddenly halted. Michalina stood up nervously with the other panic stricken people when they heard artillery in the distance.

"Damn, we are not escaping the front!" Bronius exclaimed as his eyes widened as the sounds of bombings increased and grew louder. He bent down and stuck his head through the window. "I see the German line south of here. Let's get out of here quick before they blow up this coach!" he screamed.

Bronius disappeared through the exit before Michalina and Stasys started running. They desperately tried to keep up with Bronius, dodging crowds of people in all directions as brilliant flashes exploded around them. Bronius looked back while running and waved frantically for them to run faster. In the distant horizon a line of thousands of helmeted German soldiers stood rigidly pointing their rifles at the stampede of desperate civilians careening toward them. Michalina caught up with Bronius.

He pushed her forward severely and shouted, "Run

toward the soldiers ahead of us. They won't shoot women. We'll follow behind you!"

Michalina instinctively raised her hands above her head running toward a line of taunt soldiers who pointed rifles at her chest while both Bronius and Stasys cowered behind her with their arms above their shoulders.

"Don't shoot! Don't shoot! We are Lithuanians. We don't know where to run from the Russians," she pleaded.

One of the soldiers stepped aside for them to pass as he abruptly ordered them to the nearest farm, pointing the direction with his rifle. Temporarily relieved for not being shot Michalina sensed a peculiar vigilance of fear among the soldiers as they ran through the German line. Their wide eyes jerked rapidly from side to side intently scanning the horizon as the masses of panicked refugees were running toward them. Their loud rapid breaths were interrupted by frequent grunting sounds from their throats. These soldiers were anticipating their own death as they waited for the advancing Russian army.

Chapter VIII

§

The Barn In Prussia

After dashing across a few miles through a flat barren field, they spotted a large dark house with a candle flickering through the window. Fatigued from their ordeal Bronius anxiously knocked on the door. Silence. They all looked at each other uncomfortably as the door slowly opened. A tall husky man appeared, his craggy weathered face marked by lumps and grooves.

"Who may you be?" he gruffly asked with a low husky voice as he observed them suspiciously. Bronius quickly and politely described their predicament while anxiously rubbing his hands together in front of himself with occasional quick bows. This was Bronius' typical submissive posture whenever a desperate need arose.

"My wife and brother are fleeing Lithuania from the Russian invasion. Our train was bombed and the German soldiers directed us to your farm for protection," Bronius explained.

The big man observed us briefly and then slowly said in his deep sonorous voice. "My roots are from Lithuania also," he proudly said. "You may stay in the barn tonight after I bring you some food. You look hungry."

He disappeared into the house. Michalina was elated and the mention of food made her stomach growl. She had difficulty understanding his language, which seemed to be a mixture of Lithuanian and German. Prussians occupied this area for centuries however, it was her first encounter with the colloquial language.

The stocky man who was now smiling brought two large loaves of bread and a pitcher of fresh milk. Michalina gulped her food and felt a new surge of energy. He then kindly directed them to the barn. When they entered the barn the warmth and the sweet smell of fresh hay was a welcome relief from the chilly night air. At eleven o'clock all three sunk into bundles of straw exhausted, and slept soundly with the sounds of gentle snorts from two cows and three pigs.

The shrill cry of a rooster aroused Michalina. She opened her eyes without budging and then started to remove the straw hanging over her eyes, when she heard a frantic rustling sound. She raised her head from the pile of straw and turned to the right where Stasys was sound asleep. The odd sound continued in a more rapid rhythmic manner in the direction of where a placid cow stood. Bronius was frantically rubbing his lower right leg and muttering to himself as the cow watched him, unimpressed. Michalina got up quickly to inquire what was the problem?

"What are you doing? Do you have a leg cramp or are you hurt?" she asked curiously observing the moisture over the right side of his slacks. Bronius gathered a handful of fresh straw and proceeded to wipe some brown matter off.

"I woke up to discover that I had slept on straw covered with cow shit," Bronius said with disgust.

Michalina laughed as she stretched her body realizing that the situation was not serious.

"I'll go out to see if the farmer knows anything about the front," Michalina said leaving Bronius to his project.

She inhaled the pleasant morning air running her fingers through her snarled hair. She spotted the farmer scattering grain to his chickens and he appeared to be immersed in thought. Michalina's presence startled him.

"Excuse me for interrupting you," Michalina said. "We wish to thank you for your hospitality. Do you have any knowledge of the situation at front?" The farmer's concern accentuated his drooping jowls.

"My dear lady," he said sadly as Michalina strained to understand him, "I just finished talking to my neighbor who lives close to Silute where the battle is continuing. The German army is being pushed back farther toward the Nemunas River a few miles from here." A muffled boom of an explosion interrupted the farmer as both of them lifted their heads to listen. "It doesn't look good," he muttered as he turned away from Michalina. "It doesn't look good," he muttered again not intended for Michalina's ears to hear.

He then bent down to pick up the container of grain and scattered it to the hungry chickens. Michalina turned to leave concerned about what he said. The farmer interrupted her thoughts.

"By the way, your train," he paused, "Your train was totally destroyed by the bombings."

Michalina walked towards the barn and saw the brothers arguing in front of the barn door. Stasys pursed his lips as Bronius' arms were gesturing wildly trying to explain something to his pouting brother. They both looked inquiringly toward her as Michalina approached.

"Well, any news about the front?" Bronius asked impatiently, already irritated by his disagreement with Stasys.

Michalina informed them of what the farmer told her and before she could complete her additional information about their train, Bronius' eyes widened as if he saw a ghost and dashed out of the barn leaving Michalina with her mouth open. Stasys and Michalina looked at each other puzzled and ran out of the barn only to see Bronius running into the fields as fast as possible. He turned toward them and shouted.

"Come on, you idiots! Run! Are you waiting to be shot?" We have to cross the Nemunas River," he shouted urgently as he ran without looking back. Michalina and Stasys grudgingly started to follow him.

"That son of a bitch," muttered Stasys breathlessly, "He always orders us around without discussing matters." Michalina agreed with Stasys.

"I was hoping for some milk and bread from the farmer," she said breathlessly trying to catch up with Stasys. However, the sense of urgency was real to Bronius, and Michalina trusted his judgment.

Chapter IX

§

The Flight To The Nemunas River

And so they raced five miles through fields, farmland, and forest avoiding the main roads that the German army might use, and that they were perfect targets for bombing by Russian planes. Bronius steadily hurried ahead, occasionally glancing behind to make certain that Michalina and Stasys were not falling behind. Michalina was breathing deeply and getting weaker as she fell behind Stasys. Approaching the dark wet forest instinctively frightened her, but reluctantly she increased her pace. At that moment, her skirt caught a branch, which ripped it half way to her mid thigh. She continued to run until she reached a clearing out of the forest, where she could see Bronius and

Stasys briskly walking toward a farmhouse. Exhausted, Michalina sat down heavily on a dead tree trunk; satisfied that both men were now visible across the field. The brothers slowed down-when they saw Michalina sitting with her head on her knees.

"She will be alright," said Bronius encouraging Stasys to continue towards the farmhouse. "Give her time to catch her breath."

Michalina slowly lifted her head, the brief dizziness subsiding. She watched the diminishing figures of her husband and brother-in-law approach a couple working in their garden. Seeing the two approaching men, they both straightened up and waited.

"Good day sir," Bronius said raising his hand in a greeting. "My brother and wife" he pointed in the distance toward Michalina, "are running from the approaching Russian army not far from here." Bronius paused, looking at their orderly garden. "Are you not concerned about the invasion?" Bronius asked. The farmer dressed in dirty overalls and still holding his rake, shrugged his shoulders and answered.

"Where will we run? We have a huge farm to maintain."

The farmer's wife a heavy matronly lady with a broad waist and large bosoms, stood silently by her husband nodding her head in agreement. Her pleasant, full smooth face broke into a smile, as she fixed her gaze past Bronius' shoulder. Bronius turned to watch Michalina approaching as her disheveled hair and ripped skirt fluttering in the breeze, exposing half of her slender thigh.

"Hello," she said meekly deciding to approach the group hoping for some food. " I developed a dizzy spell and needed to rest. Most likely the reason is," she hinted looking at the kind lady, "that I have not eaten for twenty four hours."

The farmer's wife felt pity for this poor young lady trying to keep up with the two men. She scurried into the house and moments later returned, bringing a tray of bread and milk. Noticing Michalina's eyes widen at the site of food, she softly said.

"Young lady, stay with us and let the men run. They will be back for you. The war won't last forever."

Michalina thanked her for the hospitality and concern as she joined the two men already proceeding on their journey. Feeling slightly rejuvenated with nourishment, she started to walk briskly through the vast plain, which felt so peaceful now. Her thoughts wavered about their situation. Three tattered, tired disheveled people walking through the open field. Where are we going? What is ahead of us? The future, she worried, is measured by one day at a time.

About three miles later they saw another farmhouse in the distance. As they approached the gate, the house appeared to be abandoned. Eleven pigs roamed loosely in the yard, obviously unattended, and only grunting interrupted the silence. Cautiously, they approached the wide open door of the large white house and peered inside.

"Is any one home?" Bronius said loudly with a shaky voice.

When there was no answer they hesitantly walked in. The entire entrance room was littered with clothing as if the occupants had gathered their items and left hastily without packing. Stasys went to the kitchen to find food. A beautiful long fur coat sprawled on the couch. Michalina reached out to grab it but Bronius interrupted her.

"That's enough talk about clothes and food," he said anxiously and turning towards the kitchen he beckoned Stasys to return. "We could be shot for stealing. We've got to reach the river before dark. It will be safer once we cross it," he said impatiently. Disillusioned and hungry, Michalina and Stasys followed Bronius, wondering where he got all his energy.

An hour later, they heard many human voices and sounds of wagon wheels and horses whinnying. As they followed the sounds in the forest, they came to a clearing. In the distance they spotted thousands of weary German soldiers marching along the main road leading to the river. Large wagons each driven by four horses interrupted the walking human line. The horses labored heavily with their heads bowed pulling heavy loads of wounded soldiers and gigantic cooking pots. Snapping whips whizzed over their heads; desperately urging them to continue. Bronius and Stasys ran to meet the line of retreating soldiers and Michalina tried to keep up. Her numb legs caused her to stumble frequently as she attempted to run. Her strength waned and wondered if she could go on. Bronius approached a soldier who walked on the side of the road munching a piece of bread. Bronius approached him and inquired in broken German, if they could join them. The German soldier surprisingly replied kindly that they could walk with him and he even shared a few morsels of bread. Taking the bread Bronius turned to Michalina and instinctively held his wife since she appeared unstable on her legs. Giving her the bread, which she avidly consumed, he then waved to the driver on one of the wagons bearing large pots.

"Please," Bronius pleaded, "my wife cannot walk well. Could she sit in your wagon?"

One of the riders jumped off and approached Michalina. He pointed to the gigantic overturned pot which could be her sitting place for a while, and with one big swoop Michalina was lifted on to the pot as the other driver muttered angrily. She noticed that the driver, who appeared to be the army's cook, was not happy with this situation and intermittently turned to scowl towards her as they started to move. As the wagon groaned and bounced along the bumpy road, the iron pot beneath her swayed dangerously near to the edge of the wagon. When the horses increased their speed, Michalina feared falling onto the ground with the pot crushing her.

"Stop! Stop!" she yelled to the angry cook who was still muttering under his breath. "I want to get off immediately," she demanded.

Not waiting for the wagon to completely stop, Michalina anxiously jumped off falling on the rocky road as the wagon started off again. Relieved to be on steady ground, she slowly stood up wincing in pain when she tried to stand on her right ankle. The line of soldiers passed her and casually glanced at her attempt to walk. Bronius and Stasys arrived to aid her.

"What are you doing?" Bronius asked angrily. "We saw you jumping off the moving wagon. You could have been killed!" Michalina checked her wounded ankle and was relieved that she was not seriously injured. She reassured her husband.

"I will make it to the river on foot more safely than on that dangerous pot you put me on."

She then brushed the dust off her torn skirt and gave a signal to start walking. They trudged silently with the line of soldiers to reach a common destination.

Chapter X

§

Nemunas River

It was three o'clock on a cool sunny autumn day when they approached the wide Nemunas River. The northern banks were littered with thousands of people who had gathered like desperate animals at the only water hole. Mingling with the horrendous crowds, Michalina realized the hopelessness of the situation. The civilians were trapped and unable to cross the river since the German militia nervously guarded the bridge in the distance. Lines of soldiers crossed over the river. Michalina's fear intensified as the roar of Russian planes descended, circled, and ascended into the clouds. Families huddled together wildly staring in the skies while children cried in fear. Michalina passed an old man clutching a rosary as he knelt alone in the horseless wagon muttering the Hail Mary's repeatedly as his bony fingers ran over each rosary bead. His wrinkled skin loosely draped over his facial bones accentuating his saucer-like eyes gazing upward into the sky. She felt great pity for the helpless old figure and wondered if the family abandoned him since he was too old to continue the flight. Michalina joined Bronius and Stasys who were discussing how to cross the river now. They worried about the approaching Russians who may massacre the entire crowd. With this frightening thought, Bronius rushed towards the bridge as Michalina and her brother-in-law watched in stunned panic.

"Raus!" Screamed the German soldier his face taunt in anger, as he jammed the rifle painfully into Bronius' chest.

Bronius' eyes widened and his face blanched in fear, as he quickly backed off, with his arms above his head to rejoin his shocked family.

"Bronius," his wife cried horrified at what he tried to attempt, "he could have shot you!"

Recovering from his shock, Bronius shrugged his shoulders and continued toward the bank of the river looking frantically around him and focusing his eyes across the river. A young man was already attempting to cross while lying over a piece of wide wood plank four feet long. Paddling with his arms in the cold water, he turned and yelled out to his group.

"You cannot wait a minute longer! The Russian planes will return to start bombing," he warned the agitated, frightened crowds as he continued to paddle away.

Watching him swim, Michalina noticed a small boat on the other end of the bank and excitedly pointed this out to her husband. In desperation Bronius took off his hat, coat, and boots then plunged into the freezing cold river. Michalina gasped and ran towards the bank trying to persuade her husband, who was struggling against the strong currents, to return. She started to sob anticipating his drowning. Stasys tried to console her. Michalina pushed him off as she sobbed hysterically.

"You should be swimming, not Bronius. You never do anything to help. Bronius is always risking his life for us." Stasys stepped aside feeling dejected and then softly said.

"Well, Michalina, if he drowns I'll take care of you." Michalina realizing that she was too harsh to Stasys retrieved her accusation.

"I'm sorry, Stasys, I did not mean what I said." Stasys raised his hand to interrupt her and then pointed toward the bank.

"Look, here comes Bronius. He realizes that the currents are too strong" he said with a smile.

They both ran to help Bronius, who was cursing under his breath and shivering from the cold while slipping on his boot. As he started to slip on the second boot, his attention suddenly fixated across the river as he watched two ladies approach a small rowboat.

Two middle age ladies wearing long skirts flapping between their legs were conversing while they intermittently scanned the desperate crowds across the bank. Both mounted the boat clumsily and attempted to row across. Bronius jumped up and stumbled toward the bank and into the water with his boots. He waved and shouted for them to row toward him. The ladies seeing Bronius wave desperately, began rowing towards his direction. The boat began gliding in a zigzag fashion and sideways as they struggled with the oars. Michalina, forgetting to breath in watchful anticipation, let out a loud gasp. She wondered why the ladies were risking their life to cross the river. She admired them as they were closing in on their side appearing totally exhausted from the ordeal. This was a small human effort of aid in this vast chaotic war she thought.

Bronius, already knee high in the water, grabbed the nose of the boat and asked the ladies for assistance. They eagerly nodded in agreement. Stasys and Bronius started rowing but the boat barely moved against the strong currents. The faster he rowed, the more the boat turned in circles.

"Relax, Bronius," his brother urged. "We have to row calmly and in synchrony."

In about fifteen minutes they reached the coveted bank. After profusely thanking the ladies for their kind hearts, they were informed how to reach the nearest city of Tilsit, so that they could board a train to Kaliningrad.

The sun was dropping fast and dusk soon hovered over the valley, as they continued onward towards an unknown destination. The dark, frigid air soon embraced the tired, hungry and wet travelers. A small cottage loomed in the distance like a welcomed mirage with a flickering light sparkling through the window. Michalina hoped for some form of shelter to escape the cool night air. The night sky poured out sheets of brilliant stars and crickets chirped in harmony when Bronius gently tapped the cottage door.

A stout elderly woman wearing a long black woolen dress and a linen apron tied around her bulky hips opened the door. She kindly listened to their story making clucking sounds with her tongue in sympathy. She turned and waddled inside and returned with a tray of loaves of bread and milk, observing them swallowing it ravenously. Michalina noticed that the lady was watching them silently with her folded hands resting on her protuberant abdomen. She turned to Bronius and Stasys as they drank the remaining milk, and observed their dirty faces and hands and then looked down at Michalina's soiled torn skirt. The elderly lady had pity toward them, Michalina surmised, as she gathered the empty cups and plates.

"Wait here, please," she said gently. "I'll be back to show where you may rest."

She returned with a lantern and we followed her meekly towards the barn. Bronius helped her open the large barn door and they entered. The lantern illuminated a clean interior containing fresh smelling hay and no odor of animal scent except their own. Delight shone on their faces, as the elderly lady wished them pleasant dreams and waddled back to the cottage, leaving them alone to enjoy their newly found shelter.

Bronius climbed the ladder to reach the straw that filled loft as his wife and brother followed. When Michalina found a pile of straw she willingly sunk into her nest, and mentally faded into oblivion. The urgent words of her husband were distant echoes in her brain. The distant sounds of bombing and occasional flashes visible in the horizon worried Bronius.

"The bombing is coming closer. If a bomb is dropped here we will all burn with the hay," he said to deaf ears. Michalina continued to fall into deeper slumber and did not care about the bombs dropping any more.

All slept deeply imbedded in the warm, clean, sweet smelling straw like sparrows in their nests. They were oblivious to the world around them, oblivious to the distant rumbling thunder of bombs, oblivious to the flashes in the sky from the fire works of war.

"Oh, sweet oblivion, engulf me in thy breast forever," Michalina's lips whispered while she dreamt.

Chapter XI

§

Tilsit

On October 11, 1944 at seven o'clock one sunny morning, Michalina opened her eyes to watch sunrays piercing the loft window. Michalina didn't want to leave her protective warm shelter of straw. She dreaded the unknown, dangerous journey ahead of them. She crawled out unwillingly to meet the challenge and saw her husband climbing down the ladder and his head disappeared through the opening of the loft. Michalina joined Stasys who was right behind Bronius. At the foot of the ladder the elderly lady greeted them happily and eagerly offered them a tray of those delicious loaves of bread and fresh milk.

Michalina sat on a bed of straw, which was gathered

next to the ladder and gratefully consumed the warm milk and bread, while Stasys and Bronius remained standing, questioning the lady for information between their swallows of bread.

"How far is Tilsit?" Bronius asked. "We have to catch a train."

"The city is about twenty miles away going south," she said pointing her finger toward the road.

Michalina sighed hearing this news and wondered if her aching feet could manage all those miles. She studied her brown boots that fortunately were sturdy and the soles were still thick enough for many miles of walking, she thought. They were a gift from her father-in-law, and he always bought sturdy practical items. She smiled sadly as she thought about her in-laws and her last embrace with them.

"We have to start going now since the journey is long. We need to be there before nighttime," Bronius said after swallowing his last morsel of bread placing his empty plate on the ladder step. As Michalina slowly stood up, the elderly lady tried to stop her.

"No, no, no miss. Please relax and stay a little longer," she beckoned looking at Bronius and hoping he would change his mind.

Our hostess actually enjoyed the company. Living alone she appeared to crave for human contact. Expressing gratitude to the kind, disappointed lady, they hugged her sincerely and began the long journey south with renewed strength. The lonely figure standing by the barn watched them sadly, with hands folded on her distended abdomen, until they disappeared into the horizon.

    The autumn sun was high as Michalina welcomed the warm rays against her face and neck as the gentle breeze caressed her body. Walking briskly through the empty countryside they speculated what lie before them and felt fortunate that at least the weather continued to be pleasant. What would become of them if the snow and rain arrived early with no warm clothing? Such apprehensions occupied their minds as they walked through a peaceful countryside. Yet pain and danger surrounded them.

    Early afternoon, about two o'clock, they reached the busy railroad station near Tilsit. Throngs of distressed civilians nervously chattered among themselves as they attempted to get into the packed coaches. Michalina looked at her husband and Stasys in desperation and saw their eyes also registering the dilemma. It will be impossible to board this train. Bronius lifted his head and spotted the rail master checking documents of individuals boarding the train. Pushing his way through the non-budging crowd, he finally reached the train master. Michalina and Stasys observed Bronius from a distance watching him reach into his pocket.

"Good afternoon, sir," Bronius said in a friendly fashion tipping his hat and although his voice belied a sense of serious urgency, he politely stated, "We urgently need to board the train to Kaliningrad."

"Impossible," said the rail master gruffly. "You and hundreds of people wish this also. The seats are all taken."

Bronius nervously groped in his breast pocket again, removed a paper which he carefully unfolded, and presented to the irritable rail master.

"This document shows that I also am a train master from Telsiai, like yourself," Bronius pleaded. The train master relaxed his taunt face upon recognizing the official insignia on the document.

"I'm always willing to help another fellow rail master," he said smiling. "You may pass to enter these coaches. There might be some empty seats available."

"Thank-you," Bronius said politely with a small bow. Sliding his document back into his pocket. "How many miles is it to Kaliningdad?"

"Seventy miles," the master answered briskly. Wishing him good journey, he turned his attention to another anxious couple.

Bobbing their heads sideways, up and down, Michalina and Stasys tried to keep Bronius in sight through a maze of people. As Bronius quickly approached them, Stasys whispered in Michalina's ear.

"I think I see a flicker of hope written on Bronius' face." Michalina did see a slight smile on her husband's face but he appeared worried.

"We have permission to search the coaches for any empty seats," he anxiously informed them. "If we can't find seats," he paused, "we will have to walk seventy miles to Kaliningrad".

Desperately they ran from coach to coach in search of an empty place, with Michalina in the lead. She did not intend to walk seventy miles. Michalina panicked when she saw that each coach was bulging with people. Even the foot ledges outside the coaches were occupied with clinging men and women. Entering the last coach, Michalina feared that no places were available, and visualized walking seventy miles. From the corner of her eye she spotted an empty seat and with joy and relief, she pushed rapidly to it as if her life depended on this space. Bronius and Stasys managed to find openings on the outside ledge. In moments, the train groaned into motion with masses of humanity filling its bowels and clinging to the sides like flies stuck on flypaper.

The overburdened train slowly strained across the countryside. Suddenly it halted with an abrupt jerk, throwing passengers forward. Screeching sirens pierced the air. This was a warning that Russian planes were approaching.

Michalina darted out of the wagon with hundreds of passengers scurrying like ants into the nearest ditches for protection from possible bombardments. Planes rumbled above as everyone clutched the earth in silent desperation, anticipating the worst. As rumbling sounds diminished, everyone slowly stood up and trudged back to their positions in the train. In minutes the train groaned into motion, until the sirens continued again and the furious maneuvers of flight were repeated.

Michalina's raw nerves were on edge. Each sound in the coach, the rattling of windows, the restlessness of people, the banging on the doors, made her body quiver. Bronius' and Stasys' hyperactivity also irritated her. While standing on the outside coach ledge, they continuously tapped the window where she was seated in order to reassure her. Frequently they climbed onto the roof of the coach to observe the horizon for an early glimmer of unfriendly planes. Their agitated movement unsettled her. A fleeting urge to jump out of the smothering train and run through the countryside shot through her. She yearned for peace and quiet and for the cool wind blowing through her hair, soothing her brow.

Michalina watched the sunset across the plains. Dusk fell rapidly; then a curtain of darkness draped over the train full of tormented souls.

Chapter XII

§

Kaliningrad

The train ground to a halt at the Kaliningrad station. Relieved, Michalina stepped on to the platform to join Bronius and Stasys. However, relief soon turned into dismay as they scanned the station grounds. There in front of them were hundreds of shabby immigrants clutching their children and belongings, while others slept on the ground. They pushed through crowds, passed crying infants in carriages oozing with pungent body odors, and stumbled over sleeping bodies. These people had been trapped here for many days. They soon realized this was not the place to be for very long. Bronius soon learned from the terrified family men, that there was a double threat. Not only did they fear the real threat of bombings by Russian planes, but also Nazi brown shirts were rounding up able-bodied men for trench digging at the German-Russian front.

Bronius and Stasys shifted their eyes nervously looking for a secluded corner, trying to find a safe haven to hide from a possible brown shirt raid. They found a small place under a wooden overhang away from the station and sat down on the cold dirt. Michalina settled against the wall of the station house on the cold cement floor and soon dosed off, only to be awaken suddenly by shouts and shrill cries. Michalina opened her eyes and stood up to see a disturbance thirty feet away. Her eyes widened in shock upon seeing two large young men with brown shirts, each wearing a large band of a black swastika emblem around their upper arms, dragging a pleading young man.

"Please don't take me," he implored, "I have a wife and two small children to take care of."

His wife, clutching the two small, frightened children looked on in horror as her husband was hauled away. They were a newly arrived family, caught unaware of the Nazi maneuvers. Michalina recognized them on the last train. Michalina, mentally and physically exhausted, returned to her place and tried to fall asleep amongst the whispering crowds and crying children. Meanwhile, Stasys and Bronius were safely hidden as they silently listened to the crying outside but did not dare to venture out. They understood what had happened.

The night was long and cold as Michalina squirmed to find comfort on the cold cement floor. Her head bobbed back and forth as she leaned against a rail and shut her eyes only to be suddenly awakened by an infant's shrill cry, or approaching footsteps, or the shudder of her body. Michalina yearned for an early arrival of dawn as she dozed off again to dream.

Her arms flailed in the air trying to brush away the branches as sharp chest pain was accentuated by her gasps of air. She was trying to reach a flickering light in the distance that she saw through the forest mist. The faster she ran the more distant the light became. Her legs became heavy as if her boots were made of lead soles. And she then slipped, falling into a ditch in slow motion as lightening and explosions surrounded her.

Michalina awoke suddenly from her nightmare as warm rays of the morning sun hit her face. She squinted and stood up welcoming the morning, stretching her aching body. She saw Bronius and Stasys in the distance walking wearily through the crowd. Their haggard faces revealed a restless night for them also.

"The night was miserable. I couldn't sleep at all thinking what to do this morning," Bronius said looking around the pathetic crowd. Sunken eyes with dark circles surrounding them reflected concern.

Stasys stood next to him with both hands in his pockets, hair disheveled, head bowed, and shoulders slumped.

"I feel it will be impossible to leave here," he muttered. Michalina shuddered at the thought of spending another hellish night in this station.

As they contemplated the situation, a pleasant aroma of fresh baked bread reached their nostrils. The memory of hunger soon gripped their stomachs and their mouths watered, as all their heads turned toward the scent. Two ladies, chatting in German, were pulling a large wagon stacked with bread loaves toward the rear door of the cafeteria. The three starving travelers had no food coupons, with which to purchase food; and money was not acceptable under the German rule. All their coupons burned with the first train. Bronius checked his pockets and retrieved a few wrinkled thinned paper bills.

"You wait here while I'll attempt to buy bread with these bills," he said and with a determined look he disappeared through the cafeteria door following the wagon.

They did not have to wait too long before Bronius returned smiling as he emerged briskly through the door holding a paper sack.

"They sold me a large loaf of bread," he happily said as he removed the loaf from the bag and broke it in three equal portions. They gulped in silence feeling temporary satisfaction with full bellies.

Bronius wiped his lips with his hand and said, "I have to do something. We cannot stay here another night or we might not survive." Looking back he continued, "I'm going to the cafeteria to scout for any information about the train."

He left Michalina and his brother standing helplessly. Neither Michalina nor Stasys had any ideas and were grateful for any ideas Bronius had. Stasys mingled with the crowd while Michalina entered a grey corridor of the train station. She walked aimlessly through the tired restless crowd of people. An odor of strong sweat and urine hovered in the air made her gag as nausea gripped her stomach. Holding her hand over her mouth she stumbled out for fresh air. In minutes she felt better after taking deep breaths of air, as cold sweat beaded on her forehead.

Two hours passed when Bronius returned elated. "I have the necessary documents for departure to Vienna!" He joyfully said holding the papers in the air.

Michalina squealed in delight has she hugged and kissed Bronius. Stasys smiled and appeared relieved with this news. He had been sulking alone waiting for Bronius, and Michalina was glad to see a spark of a happy emotion from him with the news. Stasys scrutinized the document that contained the authentic German stamp of the eagle in the center of the paper.

"How did you manage to get this?" he inquired smiling sheepishly, recognizing that his brother was always a clever schemer.

"I entered the main restaurant where the better dressed people dined," Bronius began. "I quite frankly did not know where to start my inquiry. I just stood there and scanned the room." He paused for effect as the two listened intently. "I gazed across the room and noticed two well dressed gentleman with an older teenage girl discussing something in Lithuanian. Hearing our native language, I decided to approach them and presented my predicament. To my surprise they agreed to help me."

"Really!" Michalina and Stasys exclaimed in unison.

Bronius lifted his finger in front of them and said, "On one condition. We are to escort their niece, the teenage girl, to her relatives in Vienna, since the gentlemen must continue their journey to Munich."

They all looked at each other laughing and embracing, then started walking toward the platform to join their saviors as they eagerly awaited their third train. This was the fourth day of their flight.

Chapter XIII

§

Vienna

Michalina sat next to the teenage girl and Bronius; Stasys sat across the aisle facing the two gentlemen who appeared very official dressed in pinstriped suits. Since the journey to Vienna was anticipated to be thirty-six hours, Michalina was pleased to have a sleeping cot. Making herself comfortable for the long journey, she saw two young ladies conversing amiably in Russian. They were dressed in clean tailored navy blue suits and wore black pumps. They occasionally glanced toward Michalina and focused on her torn skirt, as Michalina self-consciously tried to hold the tear together with her hand. Eventually, one young lady smiling pleasantly, inquired about

Michalina's reasons for her journey to Vienna. Michalina, feeling uncomfortable with her appearance and mentally tired from her long ordeal, answered accusingly.

"I am fleeing the Russians who have occupied my country."

"But they are our liberators from the Nazis," interrupted the other lady. "We are looking forward our return to Russia after the war."

"Lithuanian people have already felt the tyranny of Stalin before the German occupation," Michalina tried to explain. "Most people were deported to Siberia and sent to prison camps where many died because of the wretched conditions and starvation."

"I have not heard of such tyranny," the other young lady said angrily and she turned away, obviously not wishing to continue the conversation. Michalina became flustered and uncomfortable so she absently watched the passing landscape.

The constant humming of the engine lulled Michalina to sleep, until a delicious aroma of sausages made her nose twitch. She raised her head and saw one of the gentlemen slicing a large sausage and handing a piece to the teenage girl next to her. Michalina's mouth watered anticipating a piece of that delicious smelling meat. To her disappointment no offer was made as she watched the sliver of sausage disappear into the teenager's mouth, where it was chewed, and swallowed. The gentleman with the sausage gazed past Michalina out through the window and commented.

"The hilly landscape here is so beautiful," he said without noticing Michalina glaring at him. She was so hungry and disappointed that he didn't offer her a morsel of that sausage.

"The country side of Lithuania is more beautiful," She snapped angrily catching a glimpse of Bronius' reprimanding look.

Eventually she no longer had the energy to sit, so she excused herself and groggily approached the cots. She mustered the last bit of her energy to climb to her place, the third loft above. She removed her constrictive boots, and quickly welcomed the bliss, pulling the smelly blanket over her head. She fell into a deep sleep as the train engines rumbled in a soothing sensation.

The train halted to a screech in a bustling station of Vienna on Sunday October fourteenth, 1944 at 9:05 A. M. Bronius shook hands with the two gentlemen reassuring them that he will guarantee their relative's safety, as the young teenage girl neatly packed her remaining toilet accessories carefully in her small slightly tattered suitcase. Michalina, waiting for the exit doors to be opened, glanced out the window to see throngs of people calmly waiting for the passengers to disembark. The faces showed no signs of panic or desolation, just smiling anticipation to meet their loved ones. Michalina sensed no threat of bombings in this station and felt her tight body relax with this realization. For the past five days, every nerve and muscle fiber in her body was coiled tightly in preparation to spring from sudden danger. She smiled then the door opened. She felt rested and ready to greet the new challenges in Vienna.

As they stepped onto the platform, the young girl waved and squealed for joy as she ran towards a middle age couple and immediately embraced her. Bronius followed to introduce himself relieved that his responsibility was over, and that he safely delivered the young girl to her parents. Stasys and Michalina stayed back to look around the station. A flush of happiness flowed through Michalina's body as she mingled with a well-dressed crowd apparently not touched by the horrors of war. The train started to depart as people gathered by large busses near the station to continue their journey to the city. Michalina's excitement escalated realizing that she had arrived in the great city of Vienna. Her world till then had only revolved thirty miles around her village, now she was in a different world.

She turned to express her excitement to Stasys, who left her side and now approached Bronius. Stasys had been more aloof with Michalina since her outburst toward him by the Nemunas River, even though she tried numerous times to retract her hurtful words. Stasys deliberately avoided her efforts, by changing the topic and walking away. Michalina was determined to befriend him again and made a mental note as she approached the two men, with whom she had shared the most horrifying experiences.

"Dalia's parents informed me that many Lithuanians are in mass at this hour at the cathedral in the center of Vienna," Bronius informed them. "We could easily reach it with the bus."

"Maybe we could get information about lodging," Michalina said remembering the necessities of life and hoping it might be possible to settle here longer until after the war. Five days had passed since they fled Telsiai and it felt like forever.

The bus ride through the magnificent wide boulevards lined by massive grey stoned buildings with ornate trim overwhelmed Michalina. Sidewalks lined by red autumn maple trees were occupied by promenading couples and families. Outdoor cafes bustled with activity as waiters hurried from table to table taking orders on their pads or and others bringing cups of coffee and cakes. Michalina felt that she was in a surrealistic world like being in the eye of a tornado with havoc in the periphery.

The bus stopped about half a block away from a

gigantic grey cathedral aged with black soot with two tall spirals hovering over the square like a mirage. They walked toward the cathedral gates. Michalina gazed at its mighty spires, straining her neck back as they neared the gates. The large thick wooden double cathedral doors were open slightly allowing angelic voices of a choir to flow out. Michalina recognized the lyrics, which were sung in Lithuanian.

"Bring us back, oh Lord, to our homeland again," the choir sang as Michalina leaned her head against the door absorbing those beautiful sentimental words.

Her eyes welled up with hot tears and her lips quivered as her heart ached for home. Michalina suddenly had a frightening premonition of never seeing her country again. The doors opened widely and Michalina stepped away allowing the congregation to pass. Dignified ladies wearing mink stoles over their shoulders and fashionable hats with netting covering their faces passed Michalina. They chatted amiably, introducing each other with titles.

"Hello, Mrs. Aleksandravicius, let me please introduce you to Mrs. Zmaila, wife of the distinguished Dr. Zmaila," said one well dressed lady.

Michalina heard another lady speaking as she passed her, "Engineer Dzenduletas just arrived in Vienna...." Pausing after seeing another friend, "Oh, hello Dr. Simkus," the woman greeted a passing gentleman who in return greeted her by tilting his hat gallantly. Michalina smiled as she observed the Lithanians and remembered that the wealthy individuals have always been status seekers.

Suddenly, she felt out of place when she looked down at the tear in her skirt exposing her thigh. She quickly pushed back away from the crowd feeling embarrassed. She noticed that Stasys and Bronius appeared disheveled and shabby as they mingled with the crowd. Bronius certainly demonstrated an air of confidence as he gathered information and greeted the ladies with a kiss on their outstretched hands.

By their groomed appearance, these Lithuanians arrived in Vienna many months ago. The Russian army invaded their cities earlier so they left way in advance of the invasion. Michalina did not recognize any faces in order to ask for assistance with their dilemma. However, she heard that the train station had shelter for the fleeing refugees. She impatiently waved at Bronius to go since she felt like an urchin among this dignified crowd and wanted to leave immediately. Bronius approached Michalina.

"Every one is going to the Keller restaurant which is a popular gathering place for the Lithuanians. Let's go there and see if we meet someone we know." He said enthusiastically.

"Are you out of your mind!" Michalina snapped at her husband. "Look how ragged we appear. We should go back to the shelter and decide what to do."

Bronius looked himself over and raised his shoulders and arms and smiled unconcerned.

"Alright, Michalina, calm down. We will settle ourselves in the shelter and discuss some form of action there".

Michalina felt more comfortable at the shelter, since the surroundings suited her shabby appearance. It was a large hollow warehouse containing fifty cots on which were neatly folded grey woolen blankets.

As they sat on the cots planning their next move, Bronius said, "Obviously, we cannot stay in Vienna."

"What do you mean, Bronius? We just arrived," asked Stasys anxiously, always suspicious of his brother's actions.

"I mean that we should go to a smaller town near Vienna. There might be a better chance in finding work and a place to live," he explained impatiently, annoyed with their cautiousness. "Near the cathedral someone told me about a small town twenty miles from here called Stockerau," he continued. "Our money is running out and we desperately need food and clothing coupons."

Michalina and Stasys nodded in agreement. It was a well-known fact that, under the German occupation, coupons was handed out only if one worked. Bronius left them to purchase train tickets to Stokerau. Stasys and Michalina prepared their cots for sleeping in their same clothes, as did most of the refugees in the room.

Chapter XIV

§

Stockerau

The following day, October sixteenth, the train came to a slow stop in front of a small station house with a large sign "STOCKERAU" in bold black letters accentuated by the shadows of dusk. Anxiously the three weary travelers were glancing around for any glimmer of familiar faces among the small crowd in order to inquire about lodging. Darkness was approaching fast bringing the chilly autumn air. Michalina caught the sounds of familiar Lithuanian words and tapped Bronius on the arm, a signal for him to listen. In the distance the voice belonged to a young man in his early twenties, wearing an oversized suit jacket and baggy, wrinkled slacks, flirted with a young girl. Bronius timidly excused himself for his interruption and started to explain his concern about lodging.

The young man smiled and said, "I'm always willing to help another Lithuanian. You could stay at my place for the night and find lodging tomorrow. Follow me." Winking at the young girl he said to her, "See you later tonight."

The girl smiled sweetly and to Michalina's irritation, Bronius returned a wide smile, which was cut short when he set his eyes on Michalina's frown. Bronius turned his back to his wife and resumed his conversation with the young man as they proceeded to walk away from the station.

"Why did you come to this city," Bronius asked pulling up his coat collar and slipping his cold hands into his pockets for warmth against the chilly night.

"German occupiers drafted many young civilian men like myself, jammed us in train coaches, and took us to various locations for forced labor. I was on my way home… by the way my name is Jonas and I am from Kaunas," the young man interrupted his story as Bronius and he shook hands "…when a couple of brown shirts grabbed me and forced me in their truck one year ago."

"Did your family know about this?" Bronius asked.

He remembered hearing rumors about the forceful kidnappings of younger men from various cities in Lithuania, because the German army was desperate for manpower to dig ditches in various fronts of battle.

"My family does not know what had happened to me," he sadly said. "Eventually, a group of us were sent here until further notice. They provided us minimal lodging and food coupons."

Michalina and Stasys followed behind as they listened intently to the conversation of how this war had changed the normal patterns of life. The evening's chilly air accentuated the dismal grey appearance of the narrow cobblestone streets line by four story grey houses squeezed against each other. The streets were empty as the echo of their footsteps bounced against the walls. In half an hour the young man directed them to a narrow walkway away from the street and stopped in front of a wooden shed with a well, weathered wooden door.

"Here we are. This is my home," the young man said lifting the rusty hatch, and the door opened with a sustained groan.

They entered a large room containing grey, dull wooden floors and worn out wallpaper with faded remnants of rosebuds. A hanging light bulb hovered over a table whose finish had worn off and pocked with carved initials and symbols. Jonas switched the light bulb on with a downward tug of a beaded chain making the illuminated bulb swing from side to side. The light produced dancing shadows on the walls of the dingy room. Twenty cots lined the wall and bony wooden chairs dispersed throughout the room were littered with clothing. A stained yellow porcelain sink dominated the corner in the far end of the room along with a small gleaming white icebox adjacent to the sink.

"You may settle in those cots for the night," the young man said pointing to the opposite darker corner. "The fellows who sleep in those cots work during the evenings and other men spend the night with their girlfriends," he smiled winking at Bronius. "Here is some milk and bread for you." He said removing a pitcher of milk and dry loaves of bread from the icebox. "I'll be back shortly. Make yourselves comfortable," he said closing the squeaky door.

"Here we are again in paradise," Michalina mocked as she lathered her hands with a dark stained soap lying in the sink and rinsed her face with the cold water.

"At least we are alive and well," Bronius cheerfully said. "Tomorrow we'll hunt for jobs".

"Good, let's get some rest," Stasys warily replied as he climbed into his cot and pulled the blanket over himself with a sigh.

Michalina unhappily did the same not feeling comfortable staying in a place occupied by many men. She chose a cot farthest away from the center of the room for privacy, pulled the odorous blanket stained with dry dirt over her head and soon dozed off. Her slumber was interrupted with conversing voices, footsteps, and the groaning sounds of the door opening and closing.

"Who is that broad," a husky voice boomed as Michalina lay motionless afraid to breathe.

"Shhh," hissed their host, apparently struggling to put his shoes on to venture out for his night shift. "They are Lithuanians who just arrived after fleeing through the front. I offered them lodgings for the night."

The other voice continued to grumble with dissatisfaction, and Michalina was determined not to move even though a tremendous sensation of itching attacked her body.

Michalina opened her eyes about seven o'clock and slowly, cautiously slipped the blanket beneath her eyes catching a glimpse of sun rays radiating from a dusty window pane over the sink and spilling its rays further over the table littered with used glasses. A few buzzing flies loudly circled them. Michalina sat up at the edge of her cot and hearing sounds of snoring at various points of the room. One disheveled young man with a cigarette dangling from the corner of his lip, carried his cup with steaming liquid towards the table, noticing Michalina, he nodded his head, sat down and unfolded his newspaper. Bronius and Stasys were sitting up when their young host entered the room. He was wearing a khaki uniform and black, cuffed boots and an expression of fatigue.

"How did you sleep? I hope that the men's comings and goings didn't disturb you," he said cheerfully when he saw Bronius standing up.

"Very well, thank you," Bronius lied scratching his neck and arms vigorously. "My body itches terribly," he whispered to his wife.

She thought her itching resulted from her nerves, but then saw Bronius and Stasys were experiencing the same sensations. Michalina glanced down at her itching thigh and started to scratch the skin for relief producing red streaks. The rays of the sun reached her cot, illuminating the grey dirty blanket. She caught a glimpse of minute movement on the surface, and bent over to scrutinize this while scratching her neck. To her horror she noticed a world of lice scurrying through the surface puffs of the woolen fibers. She silently gasped quickly standing up, her alarm unnoticed by Bronius and Stasys who were frantically scratching their necks and arms. She had slept in a bed of lice and tried to bring this to the attention of her husband without insulting her host who now beckoned them to join him for a cup of coffee.

"Bronius," she whispered in her husband's ear, "look at my blanket. It is loaded with lice." Saying this she smiled and waved to their host.

Bronius whispered to them that we must find another room and a job.

"If we stay another night," Michalina whispered, "we will be eaten alive by the lice."

Bronius' eyes widened when he scrutinized the blanket.

"You are welcome to stay here another night if needed," the pleasant young man said pouring a cup of coffee for Stasys who was standing next to him still scratching his neck with his left hand while receiving the cup with the right.

"Thank you for your hospitality," Bronius said, but we will be on our way if you could give us information about this city."

They all thanked the helpful host and ventured out to explore the small city.

Bronius and Stasys both eventually found jobs by the railroad station. Now they needed lodging. A resident walking on the street directed them to the local government office, which they easily found. Entering the small lobby a city official was standing behind a glassed counter. Bronius approached the official to explain their need for lodging. He sternly listened as Bronius explained their dilemma and without a word, he nodded and began telephoning various room and board establishments. Michalina stood with Stasys behind him listening to the conversation.

"Allo fraulein." He then stated the reason for his call, "Habenze eine zimmer" he asked officially. However, discerning by the conversation, the landlady on the other end of the phone was hesitant to rent the room to them. The official increased his authoritative voice.

"Fraulein," he demanded, "you must accept these three persons. The war is going on and we have a shortage of labor in this city. We need workers here in order to win the war. You come here immediately."

Chapter XV

§

Lovely Room

A worried middle age woman soon arrived at the government office, breathing heavily from her rush to get to the office.

"Hier Braun," she said with her arms folded underneath her bosoms. "I do not have rooms for these three people," she angrily said looking at the haggard travelers suspiciously. "My daughter is arriving from Vienna to live with me," she explained. "She just received information of her husband's death in the war." She then began to cry, groping for a handkerchief from her dress pocket.

Bronius tried to convince her of their need and offered two hundred marks per month for one room. The landlady finally consented. As she was taking them to her home, Bronius chatted with her politely and found out that she was a widow. Her husband was a bank director.

They arrived at a two story stone house. They climbed to the second floor reaching a long corridor, which led to their room separated from the other main rooms. They entered the room and all three gasped. It was a charming room with lace curtains, two beds, dressing cabinet with a mirror, a couch, and a small furnace.

"Do you like the room?" The lady inquired, perplexed by their dumb founded expressions.

"Oh, yes!" they all exclaimed unanimously. "

"Thank you fraulein, this will do!" Bronius said happily.

When the lady left, they all started giggling like children, checking the bed and then collapsing on the sofa. Everything was so clean and the bed sheets were so white.

"We will finally sleep like human beings after our long difficult flight," Michalina exclaimed with joy leaning back onto the couch.

Their giggling was cut short when they all looked at themselves in the mirror observing the dirty tattered clothes they wore.

"No wonder the landlady looked at us suspiciously," Michalina said.

The realization came that not only did they need new clothing but they also needed to get food coupons before the rationing offices close.

With great luck of arriving at the rationing office just before closing they received a month's worth food coupons. Elated, they all went to the local restaurant to have their first hot meal. The meal was not too bad, consisting mostly of vegetables, potatoes, and small morsels of meat. Since there was an extreme shortage of meat and other food products, everyone guarded their food coupons closely. Each person received only one month's supply, which was not renewable if lost.

After eating they went to a local grocery to buy bread and milk before returning to their room. The landlady was waiting for them at the entrance and spoke with Bronius since his German was better. She asked if Michalina could help her wash the laundry in the morning; and they could have their clothing washed also. Michalina, understanding what the lady asked, quickly explained that she has no other clothing except what she wore.

"No problem," she said. "I will give you one of my dresses and a clean shirt for each of the men."

They all slept well but still felt tired and weary in the morning. Bronius and Stasys departed at 8 A.M. for their first day at work. Michalina went to the basement to help with the laundry as promised. To her dismay there were large mounds of laundry and the landlady requested that all be washed by hand, even though there was an old washing machine in the corner.

The basement was damp and cold as Michalina scrubbed the laundry in warm water and then rinsed it in cold water. Her hands were so cold that she intermittently immersed them in the warm water for relief. As she slaved for two hours, her mind wandered to the staircase of the railroad station at Kaliningrad. She thought bitterly that sleeping on the staircase there was better than working and freezing here. Very shortly, her whole body became weak. She excused herself quickly because everything was becoming dark as if a sheer black curtain was falling over her vision. Reaching her room everything was spinning.

After reclining on the bed for one hour, she regained her strength. She sat for a moment at the edge of the bed trying to take deep breaths to alleviate a sudden surge of nausea. Why am I feeling this way she thought. Suddenly, a realization that she missed her second menstrual period before their flight flashed in her mind. She must be pregnant.

Chapter XVI

§

A New Friend

The days in Stockerau passed aimlessly for Michalina. She was bored and very lonely. The cold winter days in Stokerau were dreary and walking alone through the cobbled streets increased the heaviness in her heart. She walked daily through the small city hoping to see some familiar company while occasionally sitting in the café sipping coffee, and watching people pass by. In the evenings she waited for Bronius and Stasys anxious for any news. Arriving home one day from her lonely walk, Michalina was greeted by the cheerful landlady's daughter Brigita. She occasionally visited her mother on weekends to help with the chores.

"Hello Brigita," Michalina said joyfully while hugging her. "It is so nice to see you. I was so down today but you make my day brighter."

"Let's sit and have a cup of coffee while we chat about the good things that may be coming our way."

Michalina watched her briskly making the coffee and was impressed about her constant cheerful attitude. She was a lovely lady who lost her husband in the war a few months ago. She lived and worked in Vienna.

" Brigita, how are you surviving in Vienna?" Michalina asks gently since she knew that her friend is still mourning the loss of her husband.

"Every time I see a soldier walking in Vienna, my heart skips a beat thinking that Helmuth has come home," sighs Brigita placing the coffee cups on the table. "I hold my breath until the young man turns and I see that he is not my beloved. I even go to Vienna's rail station when a train arrives and anxiously observe the soldiers getting off. I hope and hope that Helmuth will be one of them," she says softly as tears flooded her blue eyes.

Michalina reached out to touch her hand and tried to console her. She thought how lucky she is to have a husband and brother-in-law with her and began counting her blessings instead of feeling lonely.

"Have you heard anything about the front as to what

is happening," Michalina asked to change the topic.

"Not good news," Brigita answered quietly, bringing herself back from her thoughts. "The Russian army is pushing our soldiers back. I just don't know what will happen here. Let's not talk about the war. Come and help me bake a cake. I fortunately acquired some flour, sugar, eggs, and butter. We will have some treats for all of us tonight, Yes?"

Chapter XVII

§

The Bully

Every Sunday Michalina and her husband rode the train to Vienna to meet other Lithuanians and to get more information about the war. Bronius feelings about his wife's pregnancy worried him because of the many uncertainties about their future. They all wondered when war would end and when they might return to their homeland. They ate at a popular restaurant, The Keller, which was situated deep under the ground, making it a good place for protection against the bombardments that had been hitting Vienna in the recent months. It had nice décor with bricked walls and dome ceilings. Many Germans and Austrians dined there. It felt good not to look as tattered and dirty as when they first arrived in Vienna. They received coupons for clothing in special offices in Stockerau. Stasys was embarrassed to ask for new clothing. But Bronius insisted that he go and forced him to the office to get those special coupons. They all received permission to purchase their outfits in Vienna.

Stasys noticed a nice pin stripped navy blue suit, a matching tie, and shirt, which looked elegant on him. He finally looked happier, Michalina observed. Stasys was constantly being ordered and forced by his brother to do things, and as a result he always sulked.

Michalina was happy to find a wide beige woolen coat, a dress, and shoes. Stasys and Michalina, happy with their selections, impatiently waited for Bronius who could not make up his mind what outfit to choose. He tried suit after suit but was not satisfied when he saw himself in the mirror. What Michalina did not like, he liked. Finally, he selected a beige sports jacket with huge pockets.

"That style does not fit you," Stasys said looking disapprovingly at Bronius.

"I think is looks quite good," Bronius said while observing his image in the mirror as he shifted his body sideways. "Why don't you think this style fits me?" Bronius inquired continuing to fixate on the mirror.

"You are too short for this style," Stasys quickly

answered already bored with this situation and was ready to leave.

"I agree," Michalina, added, "this style makes you look shorter. You will be engulfed by those large pockets," she laughed. She glanced at Stasys who was trying to restrain from laughing with Michalina.

Annoyed with their opinions, Bronius marched into the dressing room, came out with the suit folded, purchased it at the desk, and stormed out of the shop with his new purchase.

No sooner did they come back to their room in Stockerau, Bronius tried on his new suit, and looking in the mirror tries to convince his wife and brother that he felt the suit was stylish.

"Yes, yes, Bronius, the suit does look good on you" she replied tired of discussing this matter any further.

Stasys rolled his eyes and turned away hiding his smile. As the days went on, he was obsessed with his wardrobe, and finally nagged Stasys to exchange suits with him.

"No, I don't wish to exchange my suit with yours," he angrily retorted. "We warned you not to purchase it."

"What if you did," Bronius challenged Stasys irritably. "I had to force you to come for those coupons. Without me you would still be wearing those rags."

Stasys walked to his closet, took out the suit, gave it to Bronius, and without a word walked out of the room. Stasys forgot his anger eventually. Michalina thought that he looked much better in that suit than Bronius.

As the weeks went by, she noticed that Stasys was more withdrawn. Bronius' bully attitude and dishonest actions towards his younger brother continued.

Stasys saved his food coupons and ate very little in order to stretch the month's supply. Bronius was hungry one day and stole two of his brother's coupons by clipping them out. The second day Stasys noticed the missing coupons and inquired about them while looking at Michalina.

"Why were my two coupons clipped out?" he asked.

Michalina was slightly insulted since Stasys was addressing this inquiry to her, opened her mouth to protest when Bronius interrupted.

"I did not take your coupons," he lied. "You must have eaten more than you realized."

Stasys' eyes lowered, and being a timid person, he could not respond to his brother's explanation. From that point onward, Bronius never again found his brother's well-hidden coupons. Stasys' continuous withdrawal depressed Michalina but she did not want to add any fuel to the fire by trying to alleviate this situation.

Michalina noticed that Bronius was becoming more

irritable and evasive when she tried to ask about his work. While visiting Vienna one cool Sunday, she asked how long would we stay in Stockerau since they were informed by individuals in the Keller restaurant where they just dined that the Russian forces were closing in towards Austria.

"How do I know?" he snapped.

While walking towards the bus stop, they approached a shop that displayed a few watches and Bronius stopped to scrutinize them. Michalina became anxious because she knew that the last bus would arrive soon and they needed to go. Michalina was puzzled that Bronius did not sense this urgency. Looking towards the bus stop she saw that the bus was arriving.

"Bronius, the bus is coming!" she shouted. "We have to run."

Bronius looked up and started to run leaving Michalina behind. He jumped into the bus before the doors closed. Michalina reached the bus as it was slowly moving and she pounded frantically on the closed door.

"Let me in, let me in!" she implored and caught a quick glimpse through the bus door's window at her husband's immobile standing body.

The bus driver opened the door and Michalina scampered in and leaned against the pole to catch her breath. She heard commotion behind her and turning her head saw four or five older Austrian ladies shouting and glaring at Bronius. Bronius was not responding; he meekly stood silently looking out passively through the bus window. The bus soon arrived at the train station and they boarded the train to Stockerau. Michalina soon forgot this strange occurrence in Vienna.

Chapter XVIII

§

Caught

On a cold Christmas Eve all three huddled in their small room around the radio to get some news about the war. This was their first Christmas in a foreign country. Brigita came up with a plate of cookies to bring some sort of holiday spirit. Brigita had decorated a small Christmas tree earlier and placed it in their room.

"I have baked these pastries myself and I am happy to share these delicious morsels with you on this Christmas Eve," she cheerfully announced. "I do hope that you enjoy". Michalina ran to her and gave her a big hug and kissed her cheek.

"Thank you for your kindness to bring us a little joy,"

Bronius smilingly said as he kissed Brigita's hand. Stasys smiled and nodded his head in gratitude.

The New Year's Eve was also celebrated in their room and at midnight Hitler's voice boomed from the radio wishing the country a Happy New Year and continued to speak patriotically in a breathless, high-pitched voice.

"We will fight to the bitter end!" he screamed. (He shot himself four months later.)

After the Holidays the days again were monotonous. By now the Russian and more American bombardment increased in Vienna. Michalina was helping the landlady around the house but needed to sit down and relax since her pregnancy made her activities more difficult. Suddenly, there were two large explosions, one after the other, disseminated in Stockerau. Michalina felt that the entire small city shook and was at the verge of crumbling. Stunned and immobilized by fright, she realized that the city was being bombed.

"What are you doing here sitting when bombs are dropping?" Exclaimed the landlady rushing into the room, grabbing Michalina's hand and dragging her down to the cold basement.

"They are bombing the train station," she said breathlessly.

Michalina shuddered in the corner thinking about her husband and brother-in-law working in the center of the bombing activity. She held her breath intermittently, waiting anxiously for them to return. Bombings continued as she shut her eyes dreading the possible consequences of intense damage at the railroad station. One hour passed when she heard Bronius shouting as he rushed into the house with Stasys.

"Is everyone alright?" He shouted breathlessly.

"We are down in the basement," Michalina shouted feeling so much relief to see them running down the steps.

That evening they sat in their room discussing the grave situation in this city and Vienna. The bombardment was increasing at an alarming rate.

"We need to leave here to go to a safer place." Bronius anxiously concluded as he paced the room. "A safer area could be near the Swiss border since the Russians are invading Vienna and Americans are bombing Southern Germany." His wife and brother nodded in agreement not having any other plan to offer.

"We need to be very careful not to tell anyone about our plan to leave," Bronius whispered.

"But what about telling our landlady?" Stasys whispered back.

"Definitely not even the landlady." Bronius answered putting a finger to his lips.

It was well known that if anyone fled their work posts

while working for the German army during emergencies, the Germans would shoot you on the spot.

After quietly thinking, Michalina disagreed about not informing the landlady of their planned departure.

"If she notices that we have left, then I am sure that the authorities will be notified about our disappearance. Being informed about our decision to leave, she might more likely not notify anyone," Michalina insisted.

Bronius and Stasys looked at each other to ponder what Michalina just proposed. Another concern was that they had to leave quietly without the landlady suspecting their flight.

Still not convinced Bronius continued to pace the room digesting these possibilities, while Stasys quietly sat on the bed maintaining a neutral opinion and wringing his hands nervously, as he usually does when deep in thought or uncertainties.

"Let's take a two day vacation leave and buy our train tickets," Bronius finally said to Stasys.

He was still vehemently against informing the landlady of their departure. He was afraid that she might inform the German police and that would be the end of their plans to flee and possibly of being shot. This was a very frightening thought.

"Ok," Bronius decided. "We will inform her only if

she catches us leaving. But meanwhile, we will have to leave very early in the morning while she is still sleeping. Let's take a two day vacation leave and buy our train tickets." Bronius finally said to Stasys.

After discussing their plans they immediately went to the station and bought train tickets to Vienna for February 19th, 7:00 A.M. Early the next morning they silently packed and dressed quietly tip toeing through the room with out a sound and communicating only with gestures. The three of them finally reached the door, preparing to open it, they paused and took a deep breath. Bronius turned the knob ever so quietly and opened the door. Stepping out from their room onto the corridor, they paused suddenly without a step. At the end of the corridor Madame stood there, like a flickering candle in the night, in her nightgown with her arms crossed and her lower lip protruded in a scowl.

"Where and why are you leaving so early with your suitcase?" she demanded gazing at the luggage Bronius was carrying.

"We are leaving, Madame and we need to catch an early train." Bronius hesitantly stammered.

"Leaving!" she shrieked. "Leaving," she repeated. "You are running away." Her voice was bitter and angry. "You are running away and I have to stay behind."

Not wanting to discuss this any further they briskly

hastened past her to the door.

"We left the key on the bureau, Madame." Bronius said turning to look at her as he hastened his speed. "The train will be leaving soon."

They increased their pace toward the station and after a short distance, the beckoning train whistle screeched in the distance. The screaming landlady ran after them.

"Halt! Halt" she shouted. They all turned slowly and Michalina noted beads of sweat poured from Bronius forehead.

"This is it," Bronius said with a look of panic. "We are in trouble." He said as he watched the landlady running toward them. "We have to separate!" He gasped preparing to run away.

Michalina could not believe what Bronius just said.

"Let's not panic," she tried to calm him and held his arm forcefully to prevent his running. "Let's see what she wants," Michalina said pleadingly, dreading the thought of being abandoned and to be on her own. She was seven months pregnant after all!

They all apprehensively stood still as the angry Madame approached them and in a loud voice angrily proclaimed that she could not find the key. Uncomfortable by this loud disturbance on the street, they looked around hoping that no one was paying attention to them.

"Madame, the key is on the bureau," Bronius calmly reassured her.

"It is not on the bureau," she again boomed. "You must come with me back to the house and show me where you put the key."

"Madame, our train will be leaving soon," Bronius pleaded. "We cannot go with you." She stubbornly stood her ground with her arms firmly crossed in front of her.

"You must come," she blurted loudly, "or you will pay for this!"

Bronius looked pleadingly as his younger brother.

"You must go back with Madame, Stasys. We have no choice. You will make it back to the train in time."

Stasys glared at his brother and then glanced annoyingly at Michalina. Without a word, he took Madame's arm gently.

"Come quickly." He said. "I will show you where I put the key." Relieved, Madame briskly followed Stasys back to the house.

Michalina and Bronius said nothing as they waited for the train. She glanced at her husband sideways wondering what the brothers' relationships were like in the past. Bronius was more determined and aggressive to make things happen. Stasys was the quiet and passive type. Bronius always nagged and pushed him either to purchase new clothing or return back to the house even though he could miss this train. The thought that Bronius would have run away leaving her to survive alone, made her shiver. At this moment she was hoping that her brother-in-law would make it before the train left. Again she glanced at her husband who was silent and trying to ignore her accusing glances.

Seven o'clock arrived but no train to be seen or heard. Michalina was silently elated that this extra delay would give Stasys more time. In fifteen minutes she spots Stasys running in the distance. He was completely wet, flushed and breathing hard.

"That damned old woman." Stasys muttered under his breath. "The key was on the floor and shining clearly." At that point the whistle blew as the train slowed to a stop in the station. Bronius tapped Stasys gently on the shoulder for consolation, but Stasys shrugged his shoulder away from his brother's touch as they climbed into one of the coaches.

Chapter XIX

§

A Train Full Of Soldiers

As they seated themselves in the coach, the train immediately proceeded towards Vienna. To their horror only saw German soldiers. They tried to appear relaxed as Bronius whispered to Stasys,

"I hope the landlady didn't call the police. They may be waiting for us at the station in Vienna."

"It did not seem to me that she would," Stasys whispered. "She seemed satisfied when she found the key." Michalina noticed that her husband was not consoled by Stasys' impressions.

In one hour the train slowed down approaching the Vienna station. Quickly gathering their belongings, feeling great fear and apprehension, they trudged out with the German soldiers. Michalina climbed down from the coach, her knees weak and trembling. Nervously they glanced around the station to see if any of police awaited them and then quickened their pace to leave the station and turn to a small street. They tried to be inconspicuous. When out of sight from the station they leaned against a building trying to catch their breaths and think calmly about their next move.

"We will need to go back to the station counter to find out the departure schedules," Bronius said.

Stasys glared at Bronius expecting an order from his brother. Bronius turned and opened his mouth to say something but upon seeing his brother angrily staring he quickly turned and walked toward the station. Michalina and Stasys looked at each other and then meekly followed the rapidly disappearing figure of Bronius rushing toward the railroad station. Michalina, trying to keep up, felt in her heart that Bronius found solutions faster than her brother-in-law. They watched him from a distance gesturing with the office attendant and looking at his watch. They slowly approached him listening to his discussion with the ticket person.

"But we need to get on the train to Munich," Bronius explained in polite earnest. "We have just arrived from Lithuania and a job is waiting for me in Kempten as a train station chief," he lied convincingly.

"Yes, Herr but the train is only for soldiers not civilians," she explained. Michalina gasped upon hearing Bronius' continuous request.

"Yes, Fraulein, but I feel like a German soldier. After all, as a train station master, I have let through many trains carrying the brave German soldiers," Bronius said passionately as the lady scrutinized his documents.

She hesitated again, rereading his papers after hearing his emotional plea. Obviously, it appeared that she was flattered by Bronius' statement about the brave German soldiers. She then re-scrutinized the young trio, the shy young man behind Bronius and an anxious pregnant woman, both looking to the aggressive pleading speaker whose hands were folded over his chest as if in prayer. These are hard times, she thought, for Germany and her people and sighed as she looked at the distraught trio.

"I will check with the higher authorities about your request," she finally stated taking Bronius' documents with her.

Ten minutes seemed like an eternity as Michalina observed weary masses of German military boarding the train, carrying heavy ammunition and stuffed khaki sacks on their backs. She had a very eerie feeling observing the soldiers since she felt an intense electricity of fear hovering over the station. And yet, there was absolute silence with an occasional rustling sound of clothing or a mechanical squeaking of the train. It was as if she was watching a silent movie waiting for subtitles to appear. Michalina shivered.

"Another train, another town. When will this running be over?" She whispered to herself.

Michalina's thoughts were interrupted when the woman arrived, handing the neatly folded documents to Bronius.

"You may board this train," she said sternly to Bronius. "Let me show you where your seats are located."

Relieved they followed her entering one of the coaches packed with soldiers staring blankly into space. She led them to the end of the coach to a corner where a small bench for two was situated. All three of them managed to squeeze in. As Michalina sat waiting for the train to start, her eyelids began to droop and finally she was lulled to sleep by the rhythmic mechanical sounds of the train. Her body embraced the peace she felt. The peaceful humming in her mind was abruptly interrupted with distant sounds of echoes of her name. Michalina tried to dismiss it by submerging deeper into slumber. She heard her name called louder and louder but could not open her eyes. As the voice became clearer she emerged reluctantly from her trance.

"Michalina, Michalina," Bronius' urgently persisted while shaking her to wake up. "Wake up," he whispered. "I think we are in trouble. A German officer is checking everyone's document," he exclaimed nervously.

In a flash, Michalina was back in her alert state of tension. Michalina was watching the stern uniformed figure studying a paper from an indifferent soldier. They all squirmed when the officer noticed them in the distance and was rapidly approaching them. No doubt he felt that they were an incongruous trio in a military train. He stopped abruptly looking down at what it may have seemed to him observing three wide eyed scared rabbits.

"Who let you in this train," he demanded.

Bronius, the braver of the three, opened his mouth to explain, but was interrupted by the lady who gave them permission to board.

"Captain," she firmly said. "This man," pointing at Bronius, "had proper documents and needs to be in Kempten to work as a train master."

"Fraulein," the angry officer retorted in a loud crisp authoritative voice, "this is a military train for the soldiers only. Is he a German soldier?" he demanded pointing at Bronius.

"No," the lady said meekly with her head down.

"Then at the next stop they must leave," he then quickly turned and abruptly departed to the next coach. The lady looked at the silent trio, raised her shoulders to indicate that this is how it would be, and she scurried after the officer.

Chapter XX

§

Ghostly Terrain

Shortly thereafter, the train arrived to the next station. They scurried quickly out of the car into the dark cold night. Michalina was relieved that they now be safe. Hopefully, no one was looking for them. At the ticket office they studied the train scheduled and saw that the next train to Munich would be in two hours. After buying the tickets they settled down to wait. Michalina gazed around the station and saw many shabby and tired people silently waiting as they were. As her gaze wandered, she spotted a tall thin ghostly figure wrapped in a tattered brown army blanket. His hollow, skeletal facial features accentuated his large white eyeballs flickering aimlessly in the sockets. Michalina intently focused on him and surmised that this poor man either escaped or was released from a concentration camp. Michalina silently cried for him and for many like him. This ghostly figure made her feel more fortunate. "We are all alive and still strong," she thought. Then a surge of hope overwhelmed her.

The train finally arrived. As Michalina boarded the train, she paused to look around to see if the unfortunate soul was boarding also, but he disappeared from her view. They found a comfortable spot as she sat down with a sigh.

"We are prepared to roam the world like gypsies," she whispered to herself.

Michalina gazed out the window as the train started to move. The station was totally empty and she saw how severely it was bombed. The sun was rising in the horizon slowly as if it hesitated. Scanning the countryside through the train window, Michalina knew why the sun was hesitant to illuminate this world. Ruins upon ruins passed. No life was visible. She imagined of lost souls wandering through the rubble. Michalina blinked and saw the tall skeletal figure wrapped in the army blanket shuffling through the ruins. Michalina's eyes widened as she pressed her nose against the windowpane for a better look. Her lids blinked briefly again and the ghostly figure was gone. Sadness again overwhelmed her as she saw ruins everywhere. The bombings appeared to have been recent because thick smoke slowly arose from the rubble. They all looked at each other feeling the same fear. Will this train be bombed?

Bronius broke the silence and proclaimed, "Munich is probably totally destroyed from the allied bombardments. I hope we can get train tickets to Kempten."

As the train approached Munich, they gasped at the sight in front of them, a destroyed city. Bombed buildings appeared like skeletons standing on the dark smoky terrain. Michalina stared at the eerie image. They arrived in Germany, fleeing from bombardments by the Russian army, now to face American and British forces bombs.

After successfully buying tickets to Kempten, in two hours they all comfortably arranged themselves in the seats and wondered what lay ahead in Kempten. As the trained hummed along and no distant bombardment in the distance, Michalina looked toward the passing fields. German farmers tended their farms. They were wearing short leather pants and felt hats with a pin that looked like a small broom attached to the side. Spring was in the air. Michalina marveled that in the middle of this war, people continue to pursue their daily activities. What is left for us, Michalina thought, as she continued to glance at the farmers working in the fields. Fleeing from death, they left their country in autumn, when the leaves were bright yellow and ready to fall, waiting for the wind to scatter them. Now it was early spring. The sunset was setting, spreading a glow across the fields. They will reach Kempten in one hour. Michalina wanted the train never to stop, but yet to keep going. She did not wish to face another destroyed city.

Chapter XXI

§

Kempten

The train reached the Kempten station at 7 pm, February 16th, 1945. It is dark and dismal. They quickly step out from the train and anxiously look around for anyone that they may recognize. Michalina notice a few bombardment craters not far from the rail station. They all nervously laugh to see some humor to their situation in that they are running from bombardments only to arrive to another region that is bombed. This only happens in nightmares, Michalina thought.

"We need to find a place to sleep. There may be a room at the station," Bronius said as he directed them there. The rail master approaches them and listened to Bronius' request, then he nods wearily. He has heard many of these stories from fleeing refugees. They followed him as he led them to the second floor where there was a room with clumps of straw to lay down on. A couple of Latvian families were already huddled down with their small children. He provided them with blankets and turned to climb down the stairs.

"When the sirens go off," he warned, "run down to the cellar for protection against the bombardment," his voice trailed down the stairs.

They all stood looking around not liking this arrangement.

"If the sirens start alerting us," Bronius said as he looked towards the exit door, "no way could we all in this room run down a narrow staircase with one exit door." Michalina and Stasys both nodded in agreement.

"Maybe we should just sleep in the cellar just to be safe," Michalina said expressing her concern.

"We have been here a few days now with no bombs dropping," the Latvian man said seeing their uncertainty. "The planes usually fly in the opposite direction," he tried to reassure them.

"Tonight they might just fly over our heads," Bronius replied politely.

The Latvian laughed and shrugged the concern off by

handing them each a cookie to eat.

"Let's just settle down and relax," he coaxed them. "We are all very tired and need sleep. Tomorrow will be a brighter day."

Hesitantly, they all sat down on the straw.

"One of us should be awake," Bronius said as he lay down. "I will wake you up to warn you of any danger."

They all agreed and tried to relax. No sooner that Michalina's eyelids shut, she heard Bronius snoring loudly. Embarrassed, she nudged him to stop so as to not disturb the sleeping people.

"What kind of guard is he," Michalina muttered angrily.

Since she was too tense to sleep, she decided to stay up. She was also very hungry and the cookie she was given did not alleviate her hunger pangs. Eventually dawn arrived.

Bronius and Stasys needed to find jobs so that food coupons could be attained. They were all very hungry and weak. Both of the men found positions at the rail station and given a railcar with a furnace for lodging. Since Michalina was pregnant, a small room was assigned to her. The elderly landlady, a widow, welcomed her enthusiastically.

During the journey the brothers' relationship became more strained and distant. Bronius continued to give his orders to Stasys who resented this attitude.

"It is freezing in this rail car," Bronius said one evening to Stasys. "Go and get some wood for the furnace."

Stasys said nothing and continued to sleep under the blanket. Every night, tired of his brother's commands, Stasys slept through the cold nights. Finally, Bronius who hated the cold weather gathered wood and kept the furnace going. Stasys refused to help. Michalina noticed their uncomfortable silence and knew that Stasys, on one of her visits, had reached the last straw of his brother's continuous bullying, and finally it snapped. Eventually Bronius left the train car and joined Michalina in her small room. During the weekends Michalina wanted to see Stasys and how he was handling living on his own, but her husband did not wish to see him.

Michalina saw less and less of Stasys who was actively socializing with his friends and playing on a basketball team. She thought that perhaps Stasys has been enjoying his new freedom from his older brother.

The weeks passed by and now Michalina was eight months pregnant. They heard no more bombings as the war was coming to an end. While her husband worked she took lonely walks amongst the ruins and in a few remaining parks. On a beautiful spring day she saw a cluster of blue wild flowers in the field and picked a few for her room. A young man approached her and asked her in German if he could have a flower from her. She was wearing her wide coat and hiding her bulging abdomen with the bouquet.

"Nicht sprechen Deutsche," I don't speak German she said nervously and scurried passed him quickly. She quickly looked behind her to make sure he was not following her and noticed that he was continuing onward with his hands in the pockets, head bent, and shoulders hunched.

One day while taking a walk she noticed a flurry of people rushing to enter a brick house at the corner of the street. Sensing the excitement of the crowd she asked what was going on in that house.

"Someone is giving out free cheese to our neighborhood!" the lady answered excitedly. "Free cheese! Come join me."

Michalina eagerly followed her and entered the lobby. There were throngs of people pushing and shoving behind her. Eventually in the frenzy her very pregnant abdomen was firmly pressed against the cold damp wall. Panicking she screamed.

"Stop, stop, let me leave."

She groped her way out of the corridor through a small area given to her by the crowd. Once outside she grabbed her stomach and walked briskly away from the mob. As she fumbled for her keys to her apartment her friend passing by sensed Michalina's discomfort came to assist.

"What is wrong Michalina?" she asked while helping

her to her room.

Her friend, Birute, lived close by and delivered a baby boy recently.

"Let me sit down to get my strength back," Michalina implored. "I just did a stupid thing getting involved with an excited crowd waiting in line for free cheese."

Birute rolled her eyes and tried to console Michalina by making a cup of tea.

"You have to be careful. You have one month to go before the birth of your child."

Birute was a beautiful woman three years younger than Michalina. She was slender with shoulder length dark wavy hair, black eyes with long lashes. She always wore red lipstick and blouses that draped over her shoulders.

"Who is taking care of your baby?" Michalina asked.

"I told my husband that I needed some time off for a few hours". Birute sat down and leaned against the table with her elbows facing Michalina.

"Did you know that the Russian army has occupied Vienna?" Michalina nodded her head from side to side, signaling that she did not know.

"Another horrifying piece of news," continued Birute. "Hundreds of dead women lay in the streets, parks, and homes. They committed suicide fearing of being raped and tortured by the invading Russian soldiers." Michalina continued to be speechless.

Stories have been spread of horrific incidences of soldiers of the Russian army raping women and girls as they invade the cities and villages of Eastern Europe.

"How do you know this," asked Michalina regaining her voice.

"A few women escaped Vienna and fled to Munich to tell this story."

Michalina's eyes gazed out her window as Birute continued to narrate the shocking information. She thinks about her dear friend, Brigita and hoped for her safety somewhere.

"Oh, this war, this war," sighed Michalina.

Birute reached to hold Michalina's hands.

"We will survive," she said encouragingly. "You have a good husband. I must rush to mine now."

They hugged leaving Michalina to her thoughts.

Her contractions increased on May 7th, the day the war ended. Bronius and Michalina walked a few blocks to the clinic. She was worried about this pregnancy with all the physical hardships they have had, dodging the bombing and enduring many stresses and starvation while her child was in her womb.

Her baby girl was born on May 9, 1945, two days after the war ended. Michalina, still tired after her delivery, heard her infant cry. She looked anxiously at the midwife carrying the bundle before seeing her daughter.

"Is my baby normal?" she asked weakly.

July 1945 the Potsdam Meeting, July 17th to August 12th, between leaders of the allies, Joseph Stalin, Harry Truman and Clement Attlee, who replaced P.M. Winston Churchill, decided to divide Europe from east to west. The Iron Curtain fell. East Europe was to be under Russia's control. There were 236 displaced persons (DP) camps throughout western Germany and Lithuanians lived in 113 of those camps. Michalina, Bronius and Stasys lived four years in the camp near Kempten, Area 3, which was in the U.S. zone. There were a total of 60,000 Lithuanians in all the DP camps. One out of three Lithuanian refugees survived the flight through the German-Russian front. Most did not want to return to their homeland under Stalin's rule after the war, since 40,000 Lithuanians perished under the Russian occupation in 1941. These Lithuanians were primarily teachers, engineers, economists, doctors, landowners, and writers.

In the DP camps the Russian officers, accompanied by U.S. soldiers, frequently came to encourage the refugees in Area 3 to come back to their homeland. Some were even forced by the allies to go back to their country and many of those who repatriated were not heard from again. Later, the allies realized the refugee's fears and stopped forcing the DP's to repatriate. Soon Area 3 housed one thousand Lithuanian refugees. In the four years the refugees living in DP camps established schools for the children and young adults, basketball teams, scouting activities, choir groups, plays, and newspapers. They all awaited visas to any country that would accept them. The most popular countries were U.S., Australia, and Canada.

The United Nations Relief and Rehabilitation Administration (UNRRA) were responsible for the care of refugees. UNRRA provided food, living conditions, displaced persons registration, admissions and evictions, cleaning of camp, education, and cultural and religious activities, and help them to resettle in different countries.

Chapter XXII

§

Life In The D.P. Camp 1945-1949

After the delivery of her child Michalina was released the following day. Bronius anxiously waited to pick up his daughter and take his wife back to the apartment. Michalina felt a chill through her body. She did not want to see her baby.

"Leave the baby here in the clinic," she said harshly attempting to stand up from her bed. "We could pick her up later."

Bronius surprised at his wife's statement, quickly grabbed his bundled daughter from the nurse's arms. When Michalina was ready they started to walk. He was holding his daughter as if she was a very delicate piece of china that could snap easily. Michalina walked as she grimaced bent over by his side. Reaching their home she collapsed on the bed.

"I don't feel well," she moaned. "I cannot help you with the baby."

"Don't worry, I will take care of her."

A few days passed and Michalina felt weaker as sweat oozed from her forehead. Bronius asked the elderly landlady to assist him in the care of his daughter. The landlady touched Michalina's wet hot forehead. She removed her hand quickly looking at Bronius and whispered imploringly.

"Michalina has a high fever. You must call the doctor immediately. Your wife has blood poisoning. She will die if this is not treated."

Bronius nervously handed his daughter to the neighbor.

"I will run to the clinic now and ask a doctor to come here immediately," he said turning to look at his quiet wife before dashing out through the door.

A tall blond young Estonian doctor arrived and agreed that she indeed had a systemic infection. He gave her a shot of an antibiotic Prontosil and reassured them that he would return the next day. Michalina felt that she was regaining her strength three days after her 2nd injection. In a week she felt very well and even went out to walk. She looked at her baby but did not have any urge to pick her up.

A month passed, Michalina was observing her husband's meticulous care of their baby daughter who was cooing gently while smiling at her father. Michalina felt a jealous pang piercing her heart and needed to intervene.

"I will now take over the care of our child," she firmly stated taking the baby from her husbands arms.

Sixteen months went by before UNRRA transferred them with other Lithuanian refugees to the DP camp situated in the outskirts of Kempten called Area 3 in the American zone. The elderly landlady was so sorry to see them leave. She took the little girl hugged and kissed her.

"You must visit me," she implored. "I would love to see your little daughter again."

Michalina loved the elderly German lady who was so kind to them. She allowed them to cook their meals in her kitchen and always had a cheerful greeting when she saw Michalina and Bronius.

"I will miss you and that precious little girl," she said as she hugged Michalina's daughter. Bronius and Michalina kissed her and departed for the DP camp, which was located on the outskirts of Kempten.

In the camp they were provided with a one room flat furnished with two beds, table with two chairs, and a hot plate to warm their food or tea. Stasys stayed with friends and occasionally visited Bronius and Michalina. Stasys was an avid basketball player and belonged to one of the best teams from the Kempten leagues called Kovas. Michalina enjoyed attending many exciting basketball tournaments between teams from different DP camps in which Stasys participated. Stasys was one of their best players.

Although the brothers' relationship was cool, Stasys visited them, played with his niece and occasionally babysat. One day Michalina returned to release Stasys from his babysitting duties only to see her little girl pouting and pointing her finger towards Stasys.

"Uncle hit me," her daughter complained.

"I did no such thing," he said looking at Michalina. "I took her away from the hot plate before she burned her finger." He smiled at his little niece while wagging his finger at her

UNRRA assigned work duties to all the men in the DP camps. They cut wood, dispensed hot food to the community, and kept the areas clean. Bronius, not liking that type of work, applied and was accepted for a semester to attend economic courses at UNRRA University in Munich. This University was established primarily for education opportunities for the displaced persons. Michalina was upset and felt it was his way of escaping work in the DP camp. She was unhappy that he was leaving her with her little daughter. Perhaps, he wants to leave me she briefly thought remembering the episode at the bus station in Vienna.

"How long will you be studying?" She asked angrily.

"About four months," Bronius replied. "I will come on weekends to visit. The trains are running well from Munich," he answered avoiding her gaze.

While Bronius was away for four months, Michalina tried to enjoy her new friends and nurture her daughter. She did not need to wait in the long food lines since many people allowed her to go ahead because she was with a little child. Her daughter was baptized 12 weeks after her birth. Stasys' best friend and Michalina's new friend, Birute, who lived in the same complex, were invited to be godparents. Michalina had initially asked another older lady, whom she knew in Lithuania, to be her daughter's godmother. But to her annoyance, Bronius asked the attractive Birute to be the godmother without consulting her.

She had noticed that her husband flirted with her during social visits. Months passed after the baptismal and her friend kept inquiring about the date. Michalina was so embarrassed that when she saw her in the distance, she quickly changed her direction to avoid their meeting. Eventually her friend did understand what had happened.

Kempten, Germany

Aurelia (author) standing left with playmates 1948

Bronius & Aurelia (author) 1947

Kempten, Germany 1948
Michalina, Bronius, Aurelia (author)

Two years later Michalina was pregnant again. She tried to keep the apartment clean even though she felt weak. She was mopping the floor when a severe cramp attacked her abdomen followed by a warm liquid flowing down her thighs. She was into her sixth month of pregnancy.

In the hospital the tiny fetus fell through her birth canal. She noticed that the premature infant's head was moving in the arms of the nurse, before it became still. Bronius was by his wife's bedside gazing without emotion at his inactive infant in the arms of the midwife. Michalina cried.

"Don't worry, we will take care of the burial of your baby," the nurse reassured her.

Michalina frequented the cemetery with her two-year-old daughter and sat there for hours. There were not many places to walk in a war torn city. The cemetery was the most peaceful area.

President Truman signed a Displaced Person's Act on June 25th, 1948. It allowed 200,000 displaced persons to enter USA within the next two years. Displaced persons needed sponsors and a place to live before their arrival, and a guarantee that they would not displace American workers. Refugees with infectious diseases, weaker health, and the elderly were usually not admitted into America.

Three years later, finally the refugees were getting visas to settle anywhere in the world. The most popular countries were U.S.A., Canada, and Australia.

Bronius was constantly checking the newspapers provided by UNRRA. He placed an ad to inform relatives in

America. His father's brother lived in Boston and Bronius hoped to reach him through his ads. A sponsor was needed to receive an American visa. Bronius, Michalina, and Stasys finally received visas to go to America. One day a representative of UNRRA brought a letter to them. Bronius' cousin wrote that he would receive him, his wife, Stasys, and their child. However, Stasys decided to join his buddies and immigrate to Australia. He was to leave half a year earlier than his brother and sister-in-law.

Michalina was sad when she heard that he would not join them for their journey to America.

"Why are you not joining us," she inquired. "After all we went through together during our flight. What will you do alone without us?"

Stasys looked at her shrugged.

"Quite frankly, I am very tired of being bullied by Bronius. I wish to leave both of you and start a new life in Australia."

The day before Stasys' departure, they searched for him at his lodging place where he stayed with his friends. Bronius knocked then slowly opened the door.

"Hello Stasys," he said softly as he approached his brother.

A worn out suitcase with frayed edges lay open on the bed

ready to receive clothing or mementos. His basketball trophies were lined on the bureau ready to be packed.

"I am very sad to see you go to Australia. I wish you well there." He extended his hand and Stasys did the same. "You could still join us since I have your visa for America," Bronius said as he maintained the grip of his brother's hand. "No thank you," Stasys smiled removing his hand from his brother's grip. "I have made up my mind."

Stasys And Friends In Kempten, Germany, 1948

Basketball Team, 1947
Stasys kneels on right. His best friend Vytautas, the author's godfather kneels in center.

Chapter XXIII

§

The Last Train

Finally the day came when Michalina and Bronius and their little daughter were scheduled to leave July 20th, 1949 for Bremen to board a navy ship, The Sea Marlin, heading toward Boston. They walked through the city and took photos to remember Kempten.

That evening friends had a party for Michalina and Bronius to celebrate their visas to America.

"Congratulations!" They all cheered raising their glasses. Some of their friends were still nervously waiting for a country that would accept them and others had visas to other countries. Michalina's friend Birute also was sailing to America and Chicago was her destination

Kempten, Germany, 1948 with Godmother
Aurelia, Michalina, Birute (Aurelia's godmother) and her son.

"How do you feel about going to America?" she asked poking Michalina mischievously in her side rib cage with her elbow."

"I am not sure how I feel," Michalina responded. "It seems so surreal to me. I have adjusted to my life here and now I must leave again."

"Well," Birute continued. "Remember old Mr. Ratkus?"

"I do remember him," Michalina said furrowing her brow to recall his image. "He must have been about 65 years old. He was so nice and polite. I think that he was a teacher in Lithuania."

"He hung himself, Michalina. They found his body hanging from a tree with his belt around his neck. He was dressed in his suit with his documents in his pocket."

"Oh my God!" Why did he do that? The poor man!"

"He was really looking forward to go to America. He was denied a visa because of his old age. He probably thought that he had nothing to live for."

How unfair life is Michalina thought. She was very saddened by this news even though she was reminded how lucky they were to get that special sponsorship in America.

The next day they boarded their last train in Europe. A temporary stop at the Stuttgart station made it possible for them to take a walk in the city. Bronius wanted to take a photo of his wife and daughter next to a huge lion sculpture framed by a brick wall. He lifted his daughter up on the pedestal where the large lion was situated. Their little daughter looked up to see the huge face of the beast above her and stretched her tiny arm out for reassurance. Michalina quickly approached her daughter and held her hand as Bronius snapped a photo. A passing stranger volunteered to take a photo of the whole family. Bronius enthusiastically gave his camera and ran to pose with his family. Michalina lowered her eyelids as the photographer was studying the apparatus.

Michalina was seven months into her 3rd pregnancy and worried already about how she would tolerate the journey across the ocean. We are going farther and farther away from home, she thought. Michalina's mind then took her back to her village where she was gleefully laughing with her sisters and brother while her smiling parents by the door of their small cottage observed their children. She and her sisters happily ran towards the forest filled with the sounds of chirping birds as yellow autumn leaves, nudged by the gentle breeze, were falling to the ground.

"Autumn leaves." Michalina whispered, "We are like autumn leaves scattered in all directions by the wind."

"Click," snapped the camera.

Stuttgart before departing for America, 1949
Bronius, Michalina and daughter, Aurelia (author)

Aurelia and Michalina in Bremen 1949
Prior to boarding the Sea Marlin

Aurelia Gincauskas

There is a land
A beautiful land,
Where I grew up as a child.
There the valleys sparkled with the bursting blossoms of spring,
There the birds chirped in the forests,
And songs were sung about its beauty
The songs so dear to my heart.

Having left my dear home,
Only in my dreams
I see the land of my birth
And hear the songs of my childhood.

I grew up here amongst strangers in a foreign land.
After years of worries and toil,
I no longer remember my childhood days
Nor the chirping birds in the forests,
Neither the faces of my beloved parents.

Everything, everything is forgotten.
Now in my dreams I just fly, fly
Over the banks of the Nemunas River.

Unknown Lithuanian poet

Historical Points Of Interest

Telsai, Lithuania where Michalina and Bronius lived was first mentioned as a city in written history in 1450.

Kretinga is one of the oldest cities in Lithuania established 1253. It is near the Baltic Sea

Silute is a small town on the banks of the Nemunas River.

Tilsit, on the Nemunas River, was part of Prussia until occupied by Russia in 1945 and renamed Sovetsk. Originally, Lithuanians that lived there developed another Lithuanian dialect. In 19th century the Lithuanian language was banned and this city was an important center for Lithuanian book printing. The Prussian Lithuanians contributed greatly to the development of written Lithuanian language.

Russians in 1945 occupied Kaliningrad, formally known as Konisburg during Prussian rule.

Nemunas River is the major Eastern European River (582 miles) and arises in Belarus, flows through Lithuania before draining into the Baltic Sea. Napoleon crossed the Nemunas River in 1812 during the French Invasion of Russia described in "War and Peace".

The first assault of Soviet forces arrived in Vienna mid-April 1945. They plundered the entire city and looted because there was no functioning police force. The second Soviet forces that soon arrived were extremely cruel to the female population. A total of two million German and Austrian girls and women were raped and killed. In Vienna alone 70,000 to 100,000 were raped and mutilated by the Soviet Army. They committed the largest mass rape in history.

Alexander Solzhenitsyn was a young captain in the Red Army when they entered Prussia beginning of 1945. Years later he wrote about the mass rapes and torture of women in his book

"The Gulag Archipelago." For writing this fact he was arrested and sentenced to eight years of hard labor.

The German 6th Panzer unit commanded by Dietrich retreated from Vienna on April 13th, 1945. On hearing of his retreat, Hitler was furious and went into a rage where he was hiding in his bunker in Berlin. He ordered the removal of the retreating soldiers' unit names from their uniforms as a sign of disgrace. Dietrich continued to retreat and surrendered to General George Patton on May 8th, 1945. Hitler committed suicide in his bunker on April 30th, 1945.

Kathryn Hulme was one of the main administrators of UNRRA. She was in charge of the Lithuanian and Polish DP camps from 1945-1948. She later wrote a novel, The Nun's Story, based on a true story about a former Belgium nun who was a nurse in the DP camps. The book was made into a movie with Audrey Hepburn.

Epilogue

After the Iron Curtain fell, Michalina and Bronius were concerned about reaching their parents to inform them of their safe arrival in Germany. When Stalin took over Lithuania in 1940-41, there was mass deportation, mostly landowners and other professionals, to Siberia. Bronius was afraid to write his parents for fear of endangering them. He urged Michalina to write her parents because the Soviets usually did not deport the poorer classes.

Michalina's parents did receive the good news of their survival and that they were safe in Germany with their one-year-old granddaughter. Bronius' mother walked 40 miles to Pavandene where Michalina's parents lived to inquire if they had any knowledge of their sons, Bronius and Stasys. Unfortunately, Michalina's parents never met their daughter's in-laws and were afraid to inform Bronius' mother for fear of repercussions by the Russian authorities.

Bronius' father died in 1955 and he never knew that his sons survived the war. I (the author) remember my father crying as he grasped the letter he received in East Chicago, where we lived, informing him of his father's death. Bronius expressed anger to Michalina blaming her parents for not informing his mother of their survival.

Michalina visited her parents and only surviving sister in 1962. At that time they could only meet in Vilnius, the capital of Lithuania, because of strict supervision by the Russian government under Khrushchev. She also met her sister's Russian husband. Of interest, he was the Russian captain in charge of bombing the train to Kretinga. That was the first train that Michalina, Bronius, and Stasys, boarded from Telsiai to Kretinga (never made it there). Her sister met and then married him after the war.

Stasys eventually arrived with his wife and small daughter in Toronto from Melbourne in 1962. Bronius finally met his brother after 14 years.

Bronius died 2010 in Pensicola, Florida.

Stasys died in 1992 in Toronto, Canada.

Michalina lives in an assisted care home near her son in Pensicola, Florida. Her favorite song continues to be, "The Autumn Leaves Keep Drifting By My Window."

Juozas Gincauskas, Bronius' and Stasys' Father
Seated by his house near Telsiai, Lithuania, 1955.
Picture was taken before he went to the hospital, six weeks
before his death.

Elzbieta Gincauskas, Bronius' and Stasys' Mother
Surrounded by tall grass at her home near Telsiai, Lithuania.
1956

Author's Personal Story

Lithuania again became an independent democratic country on March 11th, 1991. It was that year in mid summer that my husband and I arrived for the first time in my parents' homeland. My father joined us during my two-week journey into the past. His sister's oldest son drove us to the home my grandfather built surrounded by acres of orchards he developed. Approaching the house I felt a little excitement in making the first connection to my roots. The house appeared shabby and tired and the orchards were no longer there, but tall grasses surrounded the house as in the past. A middle age man, who interrupted his gardening, hesitantly approached us. After explaining the reason for our visit he continued to be suspicious. When Lithuania became independent, many Lithuanians who came back to Lithuania reclaimed their family properties. Assuring him that this was not the case for our visit, he quickly brought his homegrown cucumbers and a bowl of honey. He was just as shabby as the house. He wore a grey wrinkled shirt and slacks. His face was weathered with deep grooves and his hair was cut short with irregular lengths. He held the bowl of honey with his two soiled hands and dirty fingernails.

"Please," he said smiling, "dip the cucumbers in the honey and enjoy."

As everyone chatted I glanced at the door of the old shabby house. The voices around me suddenly became distant and only echoes in my mind. I temporarily felt I was transported in a different time zone in an early autumn day. I don't know where, perhaps in my mother's womb. Gazing in the doorway I visualized ghostly figures of a man wearing a heavy long coat and his wife standing by his side gripping her linen apron. They were gazing toward the forest ahead of them. I slowly turned to the direction of their gaze and I see a forest with leaves of red and gold. I only hear the sounds of chirping birds and see acres of tall grass swaying before me.

The silence is broken in my mind by a soft, sad whisper, "Goodbye, my sons, goodbye."

Author is a retired physician and lives with her husband in Walnut Creek, California.

Acknowledgements

I wish to thank my dear mother, Michalina, for sharing her memories with me. Without them the past would have been lost forever. And primarily, I would like to thank the most important person in my life, my partner, Victor Palciauskas who offered me continuous support and encouragement to connect those fragments of memories for a story to be evolved. Thank you my dear husband.

The pieces of puzzle have been connected. A Picture emerged.

A memoir is written.

I can now lovingly release those fragments of memory into the wind.

Made in the USA
San Bernardino, CA
19 June 2017